A Class Act

Walter Read

The Surrey Champion

Keith Booth

When the history of cricket comes to be written a large space will necessarily be devoted to the doings of Surrey's champion batsman

Cricket 23 May 1895

First published in Great Britain by
Association of Cricket Statisticians and Historians
Cardiff CF11 9XR
© ACS, 2011

British Library Cataloguing-in-Publication Data.
A catalogue record for this book is available from the British Library.

ISBN: 978 1 908165 11 4
Typeset and printed by The City Press Leeds Ltd

Contents

The bronze clock which was a wedding present from Surrey CCC.
[The Read Family]

Foreword

I have always had a fascination with a framed certificate that has hung in my parents' living room since my childhood: it was presented by the Surrey County Cricket Club to Walter William Read and records his successes in a cricket tour of Australia in 1882-83, commemorating his part in the England team's defeat of the Australians in what has now become the two countries' most famous sporting battle, 'The Ashes'.

For a little short of 130 years teams from our respective countries have played cricket for the ultimate honour of winning the Ashes, a game that stirs huge pride and passion and is now at the heart of a global sport. For me the fact that my great-grandfather is mentioned by name on the iconic urn and was a part of that original series and the legacy that it has created is one of great pride.

As you will read, WW's achievements were immense; he played a major part in the Surrey team's achievements over a twenty-five year period, playing in 366 first-class matches for the county, and furthermore, his prestige at the crease earned him eighteen caps for England, two tours of Australia and one of South Africa, including the captaincy of his country on two occasions, both of them resulting in convincing victories.

His record as described in this book is a testament to the dedication, commitment and passion that separates the outstanding sportsman from the merely good. His achievements were spectacular and remarkable given the time spent in the sport and reflect his ability to maintain a high level of consistency over such a long period.

Keith's input and resolve in bringing such a well crafted book together with such detail is one I very much hope will be enjoyed.

Neil Read
(great-grandson of Walter William Read)

Preface

Straight chronological treatment of a life as multi-faceted as Walter Read's would result in something of a pig's breakfast. I have therefore chosen a more thematic approach in an attempt to demonstrate how his family background and early involvement in education contributed to an ethos of self-improvement and an awareness of the place he assumed was his right in the class-ridden society of the late nineteenth century. David Sawyer writes that his birth and parentage are enshrouded in middle-class obscurity.[1] That is no longer the case, if indeed it ever was. Contemporary profiles state that he was the son of a schoolmaster, but the increased ease of accessibility of Censuses of Population and genealogical websites reveal a whole family background from his grandfather to his siblings steeped in education long before the 1870 Education Act introduced an element of compulsion.

No treatment of Read's life can ignore his prolific batting record, especially his Test match century, his (at the time) individual innings record for his county and his back-to-back first-class double centuries, but for completeness it is also important to include his grass-roots experience, of which he never lost sight, and his role as a player and administrator with the Reigate Priory Club.

The role of Assistant Secretary in the Oval office (not the one in Washington DC), while self-evidently a fig-leaf barely concealing *de facto* professionalism, was not quite the sinecure it might first appear. Allied with his teaching and administrative experience in Reigate, it equipped him with the skills of a shrewd and calculating negotiator capable of extending his playing career by a couple of years and maximising the financial benefits.

His writing and coaching complete the peripherals which form the wrapper round a career in first-class cricket significant on the field for brilliant batsmanship and off it for a successful attempt to establish and maintain a position in society.

Money and what could be bought with it were important to Walter Read. The purchasing power of the pound in 1885, approximately the mid-point of his career was the equivalent of about £80 today.

Keith Booth
November 2011

---

1   *A Century of Surrey Stumpers* p 29

Chapter One
Family Background

Walter William Read, known to his contemporaries as 'WW' or 'Walla Walla', was born in the Surrey town of Reigate on 23 November 1855 and lived there for virtually all his life. The son and grandson of schoolmaster cousin of Reigate's famed William Caffyn and youngest of six children, one of whom had died in childhood three years before Walter was born, he was an educated man who went on to be one of the best batsmen of his generation.

His father, Robert, a native of the town, had been a schoolmaster there from his early days. He too was the son of a schoolmaster, so there was perhaps an inevitability about W W, his elder brother and two elder sisters all being involved in education. The 1841 Census of Population finds Robert living in West Street (unsurprisingly on the west side of town) and probably teaching at James Price's Boys' School with eighteen resident pupils. Next door to James Price's school resides Samuel Allwork, a cooper. Then, after a shoemaker (probably; the handwriting on the Census is not particularly clear) and a blacksmith is the house in which Robert is living with his mother's cousin, Elizabeth Jelley, ten years his senior, and a fourteen year old female servant. Elizabeth is also a school mistress, probably at one or other of the girls' schools and later the same year was a witness at Robert's marriage to another Elizabeth - Elizabeth Allwork, daughter of William Allwork, another cooper[2], living on the High Street and almost certainly a relative of the Allwork family next door to the school. At the time of the wedding Elizabeth's residence was the Cross Keys in Gracechurch Street in the City of London, but she had been born in Reigate and moved back there on her marriage to Robert.

Nearby is a Girls' School, run by Sarah Brewer, wife of the

---

2   The business was established in 1806 and as well as being a cooper, Mr Allwork describes himself in his commercial literature as an ironmonger, basket, sieve and measure maker whose merchandise includes Turnery Ware, Door Mats and Matting, Mops, Brooms and Brushes. He is also an agent for Sim's Agricultural Instruments.

post-master and there is another girls' school on the east side of the town in Bell Street with Elizabeth Kelsey as Head, two lady teachers, sixteen resident pupils and two servants. In an education-conscious small town there was already the Grammar School, an eighteenth century foundation, and within two decades, a couple more - a British School in the High Street, built in 1852 and enlarged in 1868 and a National School in the London Road dating from 1859, the latter expanding its scope and advertising as follows:

> REIGATE NATIONAL SCHOOLS - An evening school for adults has been opened at the Reigate National School-room under the direction of the master, Mr Beale. The evenings for attendance are Mondays, Wednesdays and Fridays. There can be no doubt of the great benefits conferred on the people by the institution of night schools and we hope to see the movement obtain success in the borough.

There was also publicity for 'middle-class education' and a 'morning school for young ladies under the age of twelve'. All these, of course, preceded the Education Act of 1870 and owed more to private initiative than state legislation. The Victorian class structure was rigid and significant, but within it there were opportunities for self-improvement. The schools served a mixed community and an expanding economy. Also in West Street, in addition to teachers and pupils, the cooper and the blacksmith, were a surveyor, carpenter, maltman and several labourers, the schools in the area providing the educational lubrication to assist social aspiration, something which was to become very important to Walter in later years.

Children soon followed the marriage – first Robert, named after his father, in 1843; then Jane in 1845, Elizabeth in 1847 (both named after their mother whose two forenames seem interchangeable), Emily in 1849, Arthur in 1851 and finally Walter in 1855. Also, living with the family was Ann, Robert's sister-in law. In 1851, the neighbours are still the same maltsters, blacksmiths, coopers etc but not in the same order, suggesting that the Census enumerator took a different route from that travelled ten years previously. Miss Jelley is no longer there, superseded by Robert's wife and growing family

Robert took his profession seriously. He was an early member of the College of Preceptors (now College of Teachers) an incorporated society of Schoolmasters, dating from 1846, which set teaching standards and instigated a series of qualifications for teachers. In 1855, the year of Walter's birth, Robert had acquired his own school, advertised in the local press as

REIGATE COMMERCIAL SCHOOL
(West Street)
Conducted by Mr Robert Read
A member of the College of Preceptors

The School (as its name implies) provides a course of sound instruction in those subjects which have direct relation to the business of life; viz The Holy Scriptures, Reading, Writing, Grammar, and Composition; Arithmetic, Etc and Book-keeping, Geography and Mapping with the elements of Drawing and Vocal Music, are also taught. Extra Terms for a thorough grounding in Latin and French: the latter being taught by Monr Alsacer, Professor of Languages.

A string of references follows, including Rev W T Jones MA, the College, Sydenham with whom Mr Read had been an articled Assistant for three years.[3]

Meanwhile, Mrs Brewer's school has become an 'Establishment for Young Ladies', rather more refined, but complementing in a mid-nineteenth century way, the neighbouring commercial school.

Terms
including the usual course of English Study and French which is constantly spoken.
For pupils above 10 years of age   35gns
Under that age   30gns
Music, Drawing and Dancing by efficient masters on the usual terms
Washing four guineas
Each pupil is required to bring a Silver Fork and Spoon and six towels which will be returned on her leaving the establishment.
Half yearly payments are requested and a Quarter's notice previous to the removal of a pupil.

The address of the establishment is Holmesdale House, Reigate which becomes the address – and name - of Robert Read's School, so it is likely that the latter took over the buildings while the young ladies' education became concentrated on the other side of town.

---

3   Palgrave *Illustrated Handbook to Reigate*

In 1861, Mrs Read is recorded as 'Jane' and described as a School Mistress. All the children are described as 'scholars'.[4] Ann is no longer with the family; now married as Ann Stacey, she is acting as Housekeeper to her father, William Allwork in the High Street.

Fast forward to 1871: eldest daughter Jane has no recorded 'rank, profession or occupation', but the remainder are all involved in education, Elizabeth and Emily as 'Morning Governesses', Arthur as an undergraduate and Walter as an Assistant Teacher at the age of 15. The household is completed by a Housemaid and Kitchenmaid. Neighbours now include an upholsterer and builder and there is a lodging house – all symptomatic of an expanding community whose economic and social profile has been changed by the advent of the railway in 1841.

Walter's elder brother Arthur also entered the teaching profession later, but rather more seriously and longer-term in his case. He shared some of Walter's early cricketing experiences, but, unlike his younger sibling, had no aspirations beyond club cricket and took himself off to The Queen's College, Oxford, matriculating in 1869 at the age of eighteen and graduating in 1874 before returning to Reigate and becoming an Assistant Master in his father's school.

By 1881, Jane has left home and there has been upward professional mobility in the case of the other four: Elizabeth and Emily, now both in their early thirties are Private Daily Governesses, Arthur a 'Schoolmaster', but with the additional description of 'Tutor BA Oxford', and thirty years later Ann is back, but now as Ann Stacey and a widow. Mother Elizabeth Jane has died, so the two bereaved members of the senior generation have now settled for a convenient arrangement whereby Ann, now aged 68, acts as Housekeeper for the family, assisted by a Kitchenmaid and Housemaid. There are eleven boarders at the school, aged from eight to fifteen. Walter, now aged 25 (though recorded as 35 in error on the Census) is a Schoolmaster, although now on the brink of an alternative career which was to bring him rather more fame than teaching. By this time, there is only one school in West Street, referred to in the newspapers as 'Mr Read's Holmesdale House'. The blacksmiths, identified in the 1841 Census are still there, Jane Champion, the head of the household, still describing herself as such notwithstanding the fact she is now aged 88.

---

4   Census-speak for 'schoolchildren', not University academic staff.

In 1884, in his late twenties and prime cricketing form, Walter has left the parental home and moved to his bachelor pad of Ashley Lodge prior to his marriage to Florence Wells the following year.[5] Florence was the daughter of Arthur and Jane Wells who resided at Mead Lodge and the wedding is covered in some detail in the pages of *Cricket*, even more so in the local newspaper. Without knowledge of the family background, it is all too easy to assume that this was a marriage into the landed gentry. In fact nothing could be further from the truth...The 1861 Census of Population reveals Arthur Wells as an India Rubber Ball Manufacturer; by 1871 he is a 'warehouseman' and ten years later, living in Erith in Kent, he describes himself as a 'gentleman', his elder son, Frederick, an Auctioneer and his younger son, Harry, now following in father's footsteps as a warehouseman. Neither Jane nor Florence are working (Women didn't if they didn't need to - and obviously, they didn't). The household was completed by a servant and a cook.

Arthur Wells was a Victorian entrepreneur who cashed in on a developing industry and enhanced his wealth and social status as a result. India rubber was more than a niche market. In partnership with Walter Hall he was heavily involved in pioneering work in the embryo telecommunications industry, establishing a firm of telegraph wire makers which *inter alia* supplied the Universal Private Telegraph Company with patent india rubber insulated cores and contracted with the government to manufacture standard telegraph wire for the army and navy, insulated with india rubber to a quarter inch diameter and weighing 90lbs per mile. No longer balls for the playground, this was big business with a national market. For such a businessman, a dashing young international sportsman fitted the bill as an extremely suitable and appropriate son-in-law.

The guest list contained some distinguished names. None of W W's professional cricket colleagues seem to have attended - or if they did, their presence was insufficiently significant to merit a mention.

> MR WALTER READ, the well-known Surrey cricketer was married on Wednesday November 4, at the Parish Church, Reigate, to Miss Florence Wells, youngest daughter of Mr A Wells of Mead Lodge, Reigate. Though the weather was miserable, with continuous rain throughout the day, there was a large

---

party of friends to witness the ceremony, including Sir Henry and Lady Knight, Messrs C W Alcock, Secretary of the Surrey County Club, John Shuter, Captain C E Horner, E J Diver and F W Bush of the Surrey Eleven, and Dr Jones of the Surrey Committee. The service was most impressively read by the Rev S Minton-Senhouse, a well known member of the Surrey Cricket Club who was assisted by the Rev J N Harrison, Vicar of Reigate, and the Rev E Thorpe. There were over sixty guests of Mr and Mrs Wells at the subsequent breakfast at Mead Lodge. Mr and Mrs Read left in the afternoon for the Isle of Wight where they will spend the honeymoon.[6]

Additionally, the *Surrey Mirror* provided its readers with details of the bride's and bridesmaids' dresses and the presents.

The bride, who was richly attired in broché satin and wore a tulle veil with orange blossoms, was given away by her father. The bridesmaids were Miss Mabel Alcock[7] and Miss Eva Knight, and they wore dresses of cream-coloured cashmere with ruby velvet trimmings and hats to match. Master Arthur Wells[8] acted as page-boy and was dressed as a cricketer, wearing the Surrey colours....Mr Arthur Read, brother of the bridegroom performed the duties of best man.... Amongst the numerous and pretty presents received was a splendid bronze clock given by members of the Surrey County Cricket Club several members of which...were present at the ceremony.[9]

In response to popular demand, more details followed a week later.

She carried a splendid bouquet, and was attended by six children....(Mr W G Grace and Mr Hornby were unavoidably absent) ...The presents were very numerous, costly and useful: we would specifically mention... the elegant silver entrée dish from the Reigate Priory Cricket Club.[10]

The matrimonial home was 'Micklefield', at 8 Evesham Road, a substantial two-storey brick-built detached house on the affluent western fringes of Reigate. It is still there, still Micklefield, but now renumbered as 12, and then as now, a comfortable walk to both

---

6   *Cricket* 26 November 1885
7   Fourth child and third daughter of Surrey Secretary, C W Alcock. She was aged thirteen at the time.
8   Nephew of the bride
9   7 November 1885. The clock was in addition to a wedding present from the Club of £250, justified in the minutes (27 August 1885) on the grounds that he was 'a cricketer second to but one in England'.
10   14 November 1885

The matrimonial home - 'Micklefield', Evesham Road, Reigate.

Reigate Priory Cricket Club and the railway station from which WW commuted thanks to the first-class season ticket which formed part of his remuneration package from the county club. The house was large enough to accommodate the needs of a growing family which by the 1901 Census comprised Ida, aged 14, Walter Eric 11, Evelyn 10 and Leila 8. Walter's birth in 1889 is covered in *Cricket.*

> SURREY cricketers will be interested to know that a young WW has recently been introduced into the world. It is a little early as yet to venture on a prediction that he will be one of the cricketers of the future. Like his father, though, it is gratifying to know that he is Surrey born, and if he shows the same aptitude, and at an equally early age, the public will be looking forward to his first appearance in County cricket, say, somewhere about the year 1906.[11]

It did not happen. In 1906, Walter junior was in his seventeenth year, about the same age as when his father made his county

---

11   *Cricket* 12 September 1889

début, but he never played first-class cricket and ironically it was very shortly after the year of the putative launch of his professional cricket career that Walter senior came to the end of his innings.

There were three servants on the 1891 Census, only one in 1901, so there was some downsizing, occasioned partly perhaps by financial restraint and a lower income than he had enjoyed with Surrey, and partly by reduced demand, as the family progressed from infancy to adolescence.

Robert Read, already a widower at the time of Walter's wedding, gave up his stake in Holmesdale School in the same year. It had become known first as the Holmesdale Academy, then as University School, was taken over by his colleague, Christopher Search, and demolished in the early twentieth century.[12] The following advertisement appeared regularly in the local press in the mid-1880s

> Holmesdale Academy, Reigate
> Established 1855.
> Principals: Messrs Read and Search
> Superior Commercial Education
> Good French, Shorthand etc

WW's son Walter, later known as Eric, was the second of three husbands of Rita Harrison, and his son Michael, WW's grandson, has inherited the sporting genes, albeit in another area, achieving international distinction in long distance swimming. Before turning to distance swimming, he was in the British Olympic team in Rome in 1960, then for most of the period 1979 to 2011, he was 'King of the Channel', the title awarded to the man who has swum that 20-odd mile stretch of water the most times, as verified by the Channel Swimming Association. At the last count he had completed 33 successful swims and achieved a number of other distinctions, including being the first person to complete a three and a four way swim of Lake Windermere, the first person to swim some of the Scottish Lochs including Loch Tay and a two way Wash swim from Hunstanton to Skegness and back. He has also become an accomplished Open Water Masters swimmer winning a number of National titles.

At Fort Lauderdale on 30 November 2010 the International Swimming Hall of Fame (ISHOF) announced the names of the

---

12   *Surrey Mirror:* W W Read's Obituary 11 January 1907

Honoree Induction Class of 2011, consisting of nine legends from the world of Aquatics. They included Open Water swimmer Michael Read, of Great Britain, King of the Channel.

Chapter Two
Reigate Priory

IN REIGATE HUNDRED

> The king holds in demesne REIGATE. Queen Edith held it. It was then assessed at 37 ½ hides, now the king's use at 34 hides. In demesne are three ploughs and 67 villans and 11 borders with 26 ploughs. There are two mills rendering 12s less 2d, and twelve acres of meadow. [There is] woodland for 140 pigs as pannage, and from the herbage 45 pigs. It is now valued at £40, and renders as much.

The ploughs, meadows and pigs are nowadays less in evidence than they were at the time of the Domesday Book, having been replaced by outer suburban development in a town close enough to the metropolis to make it an attractive part of the London commuter belt, yet far enough away for its inhabitants to enjoy some of the best of the Surrey countryside.

There has not been an actual Priory in Reigate since 1535. Henry VIII saw to that. It was originally founded in the early 13th century and was converted to a mansion following the Dissolution of the Monasteries. In June 1541 Henry VIII granted the Manor and Priory of Reigate to Lord William Howard, uncle of Catherine Howard, Henry's fifth wife. The name lives on to the present day in the town's cricket and other sports clubs.

The railway arrived in Reigate in 1841, so the town's rôle as a country retreat for city workers alongside its longer-established one as a thriving market centre was developing throughout Walter's childhood and adolescence. Famous residents of the town, past and present, include Dame Margot Fonteyn who was born there, Spike Milligan and, from the sporting world, George Best and Pat Pocock. The name of Walter Read does not appear alongside these in *Wikipedia*. Perhaps it should. Bill Frindall was a pupil at Reigate GS (and former Surrey quick Joey Benjamin did a bit of coaching there after he retired from the first-class game).

From his earliest days Walter was a prodigious talent, being barred from the school cricket team, so he alleges, in the interest of providing an even contest between his father's school and their opponents. Instead he found himself in the Reigate Priory club side, making his début away to Tonbridge at the age of thirteen, opening the batting and facing the bowling of Kent paceman, Bob Lipscomb[13] who played 48 first-class matches for his county and a couple of years later took 9 for 88 against MCC at Lord's. The other opening bowler was Walter Money, former Cambridge University lobster,[14] but it was Lipscomb who provided the greater challenge.

> The quality of the bowling would in itself have daunted any ordinary youth, but early in the innings Read had the misfortune to be hit by one of Lipscombe's express deliveries. After a brief interval, however, he pluckily resumed, and played throughout the innings, scoring no fewer than 78 runs. At the conclusion of his display, Lipscombe was so overcome at the prowess he had shown, that he took Read in his arms and enthusiastically exclaimed that he was quite the best boy batsman he had ever bowled against.[15]

It was a baptism of fire for the youngster but he was 'fortunate enough to score 78 runs, not out', an omen of things to come. He recalls being left at the railway station 'with a bottle of ginger-beer and a bun for company', his senior colleagues having doubtless gone off for a bit of traditional après-cricket socialising. Club records include both Walter and elder brother Arthur as playing members. Both played in the end-of-season fixture between the First XI and the Next XXII, the senior side winning easily despite the numerical superiority of their opponents. W Reade [sic] opened the innings for the latter and made two. His brother made a similar contribution. The names of both appear in the playing members' list with a subscription of 10/-.[16] Also included in that list are seven members of the Nightingale family which played a significant part in the Club, both on and off the field.

Two weeks later Mr Read's school, Holmesdale House, had a convincing victory by an innings and 14 (99 against 25 and 60) over Reigate Grammar School. There is no indication as to whether Walter played, though it is probable that he did. The 1871 Census

---

13   *Annals of Cricket* p195
14   Nothing fishy here: just a nineteenth century term for a lob bowler.
15   *Surrey Mirror:* W W Read's Obituary 11 January 1907
16   Reigate Priory CC Annual Report 1869/70

records no pupils at the School (it was probably the Easter vacation), but in 1881 there were eleven boarders, and if it is assumed that the situation was little different ten years earlier, even allowing for a handful of day pupils, anybody who was not completely hopeless would have to play.

The following year, he certainly played for the School against the Grammar School, Holmesdale House again winning by an innings. Walter dominated the match with 130.[17] Not bad for one barred from the team.

Local press coverage of Reigate Priory cricket is not fully comprehensive, but such as there is indicates that Walter was playing fairly regularly over the 1870, 1871 and 1872 seasons, often opening the batting with Arthur.

The Cricket Club was established in 1852, but there is newspaper evidence that cricket was played before that. The report on the 1873 match against Petworth, in which Read opened the innings and was LBW for 16, and Caffyn batted at no 3, refers to this fixture being played for the first time for forty-two years[18] ....which means cricket was already being played in the area more than

Read in front of the Reigate Priory pavilion.

---

17   *Reigate, Redhill, Dorking and Epsom Journal* 31 May 1870
18   *Reigate, Redhill, Dorking and Epsom Journal* 27 May 1873

twenty years before the formal establishment of the club.

Reigate v United South Eleven

In 1871, still not aged sixteen, Read batted at No.3 for Twenty of Reigate Priory in a three day match against a strong United South of England XI. A fixture against the United England XI had been played intermittently since 1856, but there had been some splintering in what in 1846 had begun as the All England XI. In the first innings, he was bowled by Willsher for no score and in the second, caught and bowled by Silcock for a single, as the local team lost by ten wickets. So, the match was not a success in terms of either the result or Read's personal performance, but he could not have failed to gain from the experience of competing with the quality of cricket played by those who took his wicket and playing against men such as Tom Humphrey, Harry Jupp, Edward Pooley and James Southerton who within a couple of years became his colleagues on the field of play if not actually in the class-segregated Surrey dressing rooms.

Three of the Nightingale family played in the match, which was covered by the local newspaper, though the cricket itself received less attention than the weather and some of the locals managed to watch the play without paying the admission money.

This grand three days' match commenced on Monday and finished on Wednesday. The weather up till Monday afternoon was warm and pleasant; but the heavy thunderstorm which then occurred and stopped play for that day, was succeeded on Tuesday and Wednesday by cold winds which by no means tempted people to go and look on. And although there were a good number of spectators in the field each day, yet there were quite as many who, being too poor or too mean to pay for admission, watched the game from a long wall at the back of the houses in West-street, and whose view ought if possible to have been kept off. As it was we shall be pleasantly surprised to hear that Jupp and Humphrey, our two respected county cricketers for whose benefit the match was played reaped any pecuniary benefit from it at all. However that may be, the match offered Reigate people a rare opportunity of witnessing some first-class play at the manly game by some of the foremost cricketers of the country. It was a foregone conclusion that the 11 would be victorious; but had not the twenty been disappointed at some of their best men, they might have given more trouble to their opponents. In the first innings of the twenty, Mr Simpson and Mr Harry Nightingale did excellent service and were warmly applauded but Mr James Nightingale, who had been relied on to do something cut his own career short by the unfortunate imposition of his leg before the wicket.[19]

Admission is no longer charged either for Reigate Priory matches or the regular Surrey 2nd XI matches played there, but part of the aforementioned wall forms the southern boundary of the Blue Anchor, the garden of which provides an excellent behind-the-arm vantage point.

By 1873, Walter was playing as a regular opening batsman and with Frederick Nightingale producing some outstanding performances which were to lead to a first-class début later in the season. Against Horsham for instance, one of Reigate's stronger opponents, despite the handicap of toothache, he helped establish a base from which his team were able to build a first innings lead.

> Read and F Nightingale commenced batting to the bowling of Lloyd and Slade and the fact that the bowling was remarkably good adds to the credit of the batsmen who stood so well against it. Both were in first class form and played with great care not giving a chance until they had put together over 50, and as many as 80 were up before they were separated by Read being finely caught by Lloyd. He was warmly cheered for his innings of 27 which had been finely played while suffering from severe toothache.[20]

His opening partner went on to score 83; Reigate replied to Horsham's 149 with 173 before reducing their opponents to 46 for 5 in the brief time that remained for a second innings.

In 1875, William Caffyn, aged 47, put in an appearance in the Reigate v Surrey Club and Ground fixture where "good service was done by Messrs Read...", the prelude to a season which saw WW score 61 against Brompton and 132 against Wimbledon in consecutive weeks and a benefit match, arranged for his professional cousin of an earlier generation, Eleven Gentlemen of England v Eleven Gentlemen of the Reigate Club, each with two professionals.[21]

---

19   *Reigate, Redhill, Dorking and Epsom Journal* 16 May 1871
20   *Reigate, Redhill, Dorking and Epsom Journal* 8 July 1873
21   *Reigate, Redhill, Dorking and Epsom Journal* 25 May, 15 22 June, 21 September 1875

In 1876, WW's county appearances being restricted, as usual until 1881, to the summer vacation, he played for the Priory Club, led one of the teams in the early season practice match,[22] played for the XI in the XI v XII fixture[23] and played for the Singles against the Marrieds, scoring 22 and taking five wickets as the Marrieds were dismissed in their second innings for 34. The match was followed by the closing dinner of the season at the Grapes Hotel.[24] His achievements in the season were recognised in 'a very handsome present from the county club' accompanied by a letter from the Secretary.

> The Committee of the Surrey County Cricket Club beg your acceptance of it as a slight token of the ready help you have given to them this year as a recognition of the high services you have rendered to the cricket of the county, and also as a mark of esteem for you personally.

It was complemented by a letter in similar terms from James Nightingale, Secretary of the Reigate Priory Club.

> I am sure I represent the feelings of all the members of that club the pride and pleasure they feel at this recognition of one of their number, and take this opportunity of thanking him for the assistance he has rendered the Priory Club, which he has never deserted, although far better opportunities elsewhere have been offered him.[25]

There is no clue as to what these might have been. He scored 588 runs in the season at an average of 42, compared with 247 at 30.87 the previous year.

Despite his time being split between club and county, he became more involved in the administration of the Club in 1877, when James Nightingale expressed a wish to relinquish the post of Secretary and it was suggested that Read might step into the breach. He protested that the duties might be too onerous and a joint secretaryship with Nightingale was suggested; Nightingale was sceptical whether that would work, the President suggested they try and make it work and it seems to have done for four years until Read became involved more or less full time with the county club and his brother Arthur took over his half of the Priory job.

On the question of the appointment of a Secretary, Mr

---

22 *Reigate, Redhill, Dorking and Epsom Journal* 23 May 1876
23 *Reigate, Redhill, Dorking and Epsom Journal* 18 July 1876
24 *Reigate, Redhill, Dorking and Epsom Journal* 26 September 1876
25 *Reigate, Redhill, Dorking and Epsom Journal* 3 October 1876

Nightingale asked to be relieved from his duties and suggested that Mr Read, as a gentleman who had cricket in his heart, would be a suitable man for the post. Mr Read was willing to accept the Secretaryship jointly with Mr Nightingale but felt that he would be unable to undertake the duties alone. Mr Nightingale did not think the joint arrangement would work well as he might be let in for duties as onerous as ever, but he would prefer to have the duties of each clearly defined. The President thought that was a matter which Messrs Nightingale and Read might settle between themselves and they were then unanimously appointed joint secretaries.[26]

The duties were not sufficiently onerous to prevent the newly-elected joint secretary from having another successful season on the field. Against Richmond, he scored 76 out of 146, then took five wickets as the visitors collapsed to 48 all out. He had 44 against Mitcham and in the same match 'threw out' James Southerton, 41 not out in a first innings win against Guildford and shared the only significant partnership in a first innings defeat by the Brunswick (Brighton) Club. 64 against the Bluemantles (Tunbridge Wells) followed. During this match, a new awning was installed on the pavilion, the President, Treasurer and Hon Secs distributing circulars inviting subscriptions to the cost. Then, after going off to play for the county in the summer vacation, he scored 68 against Dorking in September and 77 in the return fixture against Brighton Brunswick on the county ground. His father was included in the guests at the Mayor's banquet in October.[27]

Expanding Horizons

By 1883, ten years after Read's début for the county side, the Club had extended its horizons beyond cricket and had become a sporting and social centre for the town, and a sort of 'Open Day' in March of that year publicised its facilities for football, tennis and bowls.

PRIORY CRICKET CLUB

The sunny afternoon of Saturday last induced many to wend their way to the Priory Ground and it was gratifying to see how readily the advantages afforded by this ground were embraced.

---

26   *Reigate, Redhill, Dorking and Epsom Journal*   20 March 1877
27   *Reigate, Redhill, Dorking and Epsom Journal*   5 19 June, 3 24 July,
     4 11 September, 30 October 1877

A well-contested football match was played in the field (kindly lent by Mr Hare) adjoining between several youngsters, whose play bids fair to keep up the future of the football club. On the two well prepared tennis courts several sets were played in which some of the fair sex took part. The newly-made bowling green received a fair share of patronage, while many a well-known representative of Reigate cricket strutted about the level longing no doubt to again handle the willow and trundle the leather; but though a warm bright sun was shining, a chilly north-easter could not fail to remind him that his time was not yet come. We noticed that the turf which has been relaid is rapidly growing together and no doubt some excellent wickets will be obtained for the matches in the ensuing season. We also observed that the pavilion is being thoroughly painted and re-decorated. As we stated in our last, this popular club deserves the support it receives, and the committee evidently shows an anxiety to meet the necessities and requirements of this increasing neighbourhood.[28]

A letter to the Editor in the same edition of the newspaper complains about rail services *(plus ça change?)* and mentions the population of the town as 18,000, so by this time it is well established and expanding, mainly as a result of the advent of the railway. The Club continued to expand in proportion: a membership of 200 in 1881 had become 230 the following year and it continued to increase. A 2nd XI was established in 1883 and new Joint Secretary, Walter Read, commented on what he saw as an ideal and complementary social mix, the gentlemen providing the funds and the working classes the cricketers.[29] His younger brother transcended that boundary. He was and remained a gentleman, but he could play a bit.

Notwithstanding his rapid rise through county and international cricket, WW never forgot his roots, firmly embedded in the turf of Reigate Priory Cricket Club. Not only did he continue as a playing member, but also played an active part in the administration and politics of the club first, as joint secretary, then captain, dealing with the detail of fund-raising, petty rivalries with the other club in the town – Reigate Hill, objections to the fixture list... small time stuff, but all too familiar to anyone who has been involved in the administration of a cricket club.

---

28 *Reigate, Redhill, Dorking and Epsom Journal* 6 March 1883
29 *Reigate, Redhill, Dorking and Epsom Journal* 22 August 1882 – but 2nd XI established in 1883

The 'Reigate Week'

However, notwithstanding the auxiliary and extraneous activities, Reigate Priory remained primarily a cricket club, an ambitious one with aspirations to host a county fixture during its week. Despite approving noises from Surrey, it was never likely to happen: when conflict arose Read, bread buttered by the county side, supported the county's views against those of the club.

The fixture list for 1871, in addition to the match against the United South of England XI, had a dozen fixtures, two of two days against Lewes Priory, home and away, and the remaining ten of one day. The length of the list and the membership was to grow gradually through the 1870s, until in imitation if not emulation of Canterbury and Tunbridge Wells, 1879 saw a cricket week inaugurated and repeated the following year with matches against Guildford, Brighton Brunswick and the Gentlemen of Surrey, and a two-dayer against MCC.

> From its lengthened cricket fame, the central position in a beautiful county, rich with lovely scenery, of the town to which it belongs, the possession of one of the best and most picturesque grounds to be found for miles around, and with more than average strength of talent, few other clubs have a greater claim to what in several centres of our national game has become a recognised institution – namely a "Cricket Week" – than the old-established Reigate Priory. Albeit without an Earl of Sheffield or a Lord Harris as its mainstay, the club has always been widely known and popular, but it was not until last year that the executive attempted following in the footsteps of Canterbury and Tunbridge Wells.[30]

Clause analysis of that contorted piece of Victorian journalism presents a challenge, but the enthusiasm cannot be questioned. Read was to record scores of 87, 30, 55 and 21. Integral to the success of 'cricket week' was the patronage and the social side both during play and off the field at the annual dinner.

James Nightingale and Walter Read, as Joint Secretaries had been heavily involved in the organisation and securing what nowadays would be called 'sponsorship'. To set a good example, Read's sisters presented a flag to the club.

> A large group of noblemen and gentlemen have consented to act as patrons. For a long time past Mr James Nightingale and

---

30   *Reigate, Redhill, Dorking and Epsom Journal* 27 July 1880

his coadjutor Mr W.W.Read have laboured assiduously in the important undertaking and only fine weather was needed to crown the success of their efforts.[31]

The Club was always willing to publicise Read's involvement with it, particularly with the first 'week' now firmly fixed in the calendar. At the Annual General Meeting in 1879, his being an important part of the 'week' was mentioned and the President went on to report a conversation with Mr Frederick Gale.

....he asked him what he thought of their Reigate cricketer and he replied "without exception the best bat in England." Therefore Reigate stood out pre-eminently in sending a man to do battle for his county worthy of the name of a Reigatonian, of whom they ought to feel justly proud, not only for his prowess in the field, but for the great assistance he rendered this club.[32]

For 1881, the fixtures were modified, the Stock Exchange and Old Brucians replacing Guildford and Brighton Brunswick: the matches against MCC and the Gentlemen of Surrey remained. Because of county commitments, Read played in only the last of these when 'Mr Read got out very unfortunately; he played a ball very hard into the blocking hole, and it going back, went into the stumps.'[33]

The dinner, which was at this stage an integral part of the week, was characterised by the usual mutual flattery with WW very much at its centre. Firstly, Reigate President, George Carter-Morrison:

Their friend, Mr W.W. Read of whom as a cricketer Reigate was so justly proud, made some splendid hits while he was at the wicket, and though Mr Read was present he would say before his face what a gentleman had recently told him – that he considered him one of the best bats in England at the present time (applause). Having sent out such men as Caffyn and Mr Read, was it not natural and fair that Reigate should keep up its cricketing prestige? He believed that cricket was indigenous to the people of Reigate and that Reigatonians could not help being cricketers.

Wildman Cattley, Treasurer of the county club added –

Mr Read was one of the best cricketers of the day, and if they had seen his two innings at Maidstone on Monday and Tuesday, they would have been proud of him indeed.

31 *Reigate, Redhill, Dorking and Epsom Journal* 22 July 1879
32 *Reigate, Redhill, Dorking and Epsom Journal* 1 April 1879
33 *Reigate, Redhill, Dorking and Epsom Journal* 2 August 1881

In a 203-run win, he had scored 42 and 160, and keeping wicket, taken a couple of catches and made a stumping. Although captain of the Club at Reigate and on the committee in 1882, he played for them very little. His brother, Arthur had taken over as Joint Secretary with James Nightingale, but the time was coming when Walter's commitment to the Priory Club would be superseded by that to the county and to England. He was, however, sufficiently valued by the club to be presented with 'a gold watch and chain, valued at nearly £70, a present from the members which I greatly value.'[34]

A press advertisement for the week indicates a progression to three two-day matches, against MCC, Gentleman of Surrey and Kennington Park. At the dinner that year, Read felt obliged to defend himself against what he perceived to be unjust accusations.

> MR W.W. READ responded first, by saying that he always tried to do what he could for the Priory Club and to further cricket in the neighbourhood, and he repudiated a suggestion that had reached his ears, that the cricket week was established in order that his friends might come down there and play. The playing members of the club had so increased that a cricket week was absolutely necessary to give them all an opportunity of playing during the season.

Within a few weeks of the end of the 1882 season, Walter was off to Australia with Ivo Bligh, and his appointment as Assistant Secretary at Surrey in 1881 and *ipso facto* as a full-time player with the county meant the balance between club and county had already changed. In the debate between Reigate and Surrey as to whether part of cricket week might be devoted to a county fixture he was firmly on the side of the county which took the view that it should not.

The 'week' continued to thrive in the early 1880s and when not required by the county, Read was a regular participant. In 1882 the Club had played MCC, Gentlemen of Surrey and Kempton Park, three two-day matches and part of a now fairly regular pattern, but because of diminished support and frustration at not being able to obtain a county fixture it was discontinued not long afterwards, then resurrected on a grander scale with more distinguished participants and quasi-first-class matches.

---

34   *Annals of Cricket* p 169
      Reigate, Redhill, Dorking and Epsom Journal

The 1883 week seems to have been a success in terms of the quality of cricket and of the spectator interest it attracted, and the extensive local press coverage includes fulsome praise of Read in his first summer back at Surrey and Reigate after the 1882/83 Bligh tour of Australia. However the half promises given by club officials about bringing a county match to Reigate turned out to be hollow, arising from the hot air generated in the mutually congratulatory atmosphere of the club dinner.

In summarising the 'week' of 1883 we may say irrespective of the weather that it was a great success. The interest throughout was keen, the cricket was of the highest class and the contests were witnessed by a more appreciative and numerous assembly than in previous years.

> The prospect of a county match being arranged to take place at Reigate will, as a matter of course, bring the game prominently before the public and when the Priory Club are able to secure the advocacy of the President, Treasurer and Secretary of the County Club to such a fixture we have no doubt it will come off.

It never did.

> In conclusion we can only trust that the Priory Club may continue to prosper and receive the support it deserves and that we may record the future doings of "the week" as more successful, and increasing in importance year-by-year.

The press report reflected the hyperbole which permeated the dinner. Arthur Read was unable to be present because of a serious illness, but his younger brother was eulogised. Dr Jones, a Surrey committee heavyweight, asked – optimistically perhaps – why Reigate should not emulate and be as successful as Canterbury, then continued...

> Dr Jones proposed "The health of Mr W.W.Read". There was no man in the cricket field more esteemed, more liked, more honoured, and more loved than him.

> MR READ who was warmly received spoke of the kind reception he had met when in Australia and thanked them heartily for the way they received his name.

Lord Monson, President of Surrey, continued in the same vein.

> That town of Reigate, with very few intervals, with very few

exceptions, had generally had a representative in the county eleven. He recalled the days of Caffyn.[35]

Now they had a cricketer who perhaps some of those present might think exceeded Caffyn, and who certainly was Caffyn's equal – Mr W W Read (applause) who was able to go away on his campaign in a distant land and by the care he had always taken of his health, to show a bold front to the cricketers there. He hoped that for many years to come they would have the pleasure and honour of owning Mr Read as one of the champion players of England and they were all proud to think he belonged to that old town of Reigate.[36]

By the time of the 1884 Annual General Meeting it had become clear that the county had no intention of honouring their half-promise to play a fixture at Reigate and there were suggestions that, if not the 'week', then certainly the dinner might be discontinued on the grounds of the expense and the fact that, apart from the President and the Treasurer, it was largely unpatronised by the Surrey Club. Read, now in the county rather than the club camp, amid some objections, put what he perceived to be the county's pragmatic, practical and pecuniary viewpoint, though he was at pains to emphasise, he was not speaking 'officially'.

The Committee were most anxious that a county match should be played at Reigate; their chief reason for declining was that they feared such an act would establish a precedent which would be taken advantage of by Guildford, Dorking and other large towns. That naturally would involve a great pecuniary loss on matches played away from the Oval; and the County Club felt they were perfectly justified in refusing the application. [37]

Dorking never did materialise, though he was presciently correct about Guildford which became a Surrey outground in 1938 and, apart from the war years, remained its principal one until 2003 when Whitgift School was added to a very short list of first-class venues in Surrey. Sponsorship has cushioned the cost of playing away from The Oval. Whether that will continue as recession and depression begin to bite is a matter for speculation. Certainly the trend among counties is now not to take cricket to an increasingly

35 William Caffyn (1828 -1919), professional cricketer, one of the leading batsmen of his time, born and bred in Reigate and a cousin of Read.
36 *Reigate, Redhill, Dorking and Epsom Journal* 7 August 1883
37 *Reigate, Redhill, Dorking and Epsom Journal* 12 April 1884

motorised public, but to concentrate on improving facilities at headquarters with only a limited number of outground fixtures.

The only Surrey first-class match at Reigate was against Oxford University in 1909 (notwithstanding the fact that there was a Championship match against Lancashire at The Oval running simultaneously). Unsurprisingly perhaps, Surrey lost by a huge margin – an innings and 98 runs after the University had taken their innings into the second day and racked up 577 – so not a great deal wrong with the pitch. John Shuter had emerged from a fifteen year retirement to captain the side at the age of 54. No player older than that has appeared in a first-class match for Surrey before or since. H.D.G.Leveson-Gower's XI played a handful of first-class matches against the South African touring side and Oxford University in the 20s and 30s, but it has never been other than a very occasional first-class venue, although it now regularly hosts Surrey's 2nd XI.

Cricket week did eventually go ahead in 1884, apparently with some success, partly due to Read's intervention.

> The "week" this year is equal in most respects, superior in some to those that have preceded it. It has been favoured, for example with glorious weather, with a capital "wicket", the new ground having come up to the sanguine expectations regarding it with the presence of one of the far-famed Australians, in the person of Mr Cooper whose services were secured through the intervention of Mr W.W. Read, with a distinguished list of patrons and patronesses and with a series of matches, equal in interest to all that have gone before.[38]

Read was instrumental in organising a Reigate and District v Surrey earlier in the season,[39] but the realisation that the week would not be enhanced by a first-class county match resulted in a diminution of interest which along with the expense of the exercise led to its discontinuation a couple of years later.

In its obituary of Read, the *Surrey Mirror* [40]credits him with the inauguration of the Reigate Cricket Week. What it does not say is that he actually did it twice, in 1879 and again in 1893, and although he played a significant part in those early 'weeks' from 1879 to 1885, it is with the resurrected week and the international stars it brought to Reigate with which he is most strongly

---

38   *Surrey Mirror* 9 August 1884
39   *Surrey Mirror* 23 April 1884
40   11 January 1907

associated.

In 1892 Read's XI had played Sixteen of Reigate and the Club were encouraged to be more ambitious. The following season saw the first of the end-of-season jollies, W.W.Read's XI v W.G.Grace's XI. On this occasion it was a two-day affair; two years later it would, according to *Cricket*[41] be extended to three, though *Cricket Archive* records it as a two-day match. Although none of the matches were granted first-class status, they attracted – maybe the money helped– the leading players of the day

> ..the committee were encouraged to try another fixture this year on a more elaborate scale. They were fortunate enough to second the active assistance of WG and his personal influence added to that of W.W.Read naturally had the effect of collecting some of the best cricketing talent in the country.

> The local public had particularly good reason too, to be pleased, as in addition to WG's fine innings on the first day, WW who was born and has lived, with the exception of a very

W.W.Read's XI v W.G.Grace's XI at Reigate, 1894.
[Reigate Priory Cricket Club]

41   19 September 1895
42   *Cricket* 21 September 1893

short break, all his life in Reigate, gave the spectators an equal treat in the shape of vigorous batting on the second day.[42]

Grace had 135 in an hour and a half, Read 112 in a similar length of time, albeit without having to face any fast bowling. An end-of season club pitch was clearly below the standard to which most of the players had been accustomed at most first-class venues during the season and there seems to have been a mutual agreement to prohibit such a form of attack in a friendly match.

> The annual match arranged at Reigate by Mr. W W Read was not remarkable for any such sensational innings as was played last year by Mr. Brann, but it enabled WG and WW to finish up their season's batting in a triumphant manner by each scoring a century. Owing to the dangerous state of the wicket, fast bowling was not allowed.[43]

Off the field too, the event appears to have been a success.

> On Friday evening, the cricketers were entertained to dinner at the Town Hall by the Reigate Priory Club. Mr C A Hardman, the president was in the chair, supported by a company of nearly two hundred. In addition to the majority of the players, there were present – the High Sheriff of Surrey, Mr J Colman, a member of the Committee of the Surrey CC; Mr H Cubitt, MP for mid-Surrey; Sir Trevor Lawrence, Bart; the Secretary of Surrey County CC, the Mayor of Reigate and other local notabilities.[44]

The exercise was repeated the following year, but on a somewhat larger scale as 'the town was prettily illuminated on the same night in honour of the occasion'.[45]

Football and other sports.

Various profiles of Walter Read mention his proficiency at other sports – football, walking, skating and billiards.[46] Of the latter three, no mention has been found. Maybe they are from the same - possibly erroneous - source It's by no means impossible: not all sporting events were reported in the press and he was a competent all-round sportsman, taking part in and helping to organise and participate in the annual athletic sports at the Priory Ground under the aegis of the 5th Surrey Rifle Volunteers.

---

43   *Chats on the Cricket Field* p 455
44   *Cricket* 21 September 1893
45   *Cricket* 20 September 1894
46   *Cricket* 19 April 1883

In 1879 he was third in the 440 yards 'over three flights of hurdles' and, as Prvt W.W.Read, second in the 300 yards race 'in full uniform'.[47] Maybe not in the C.B.Fry league as an all-round sportsman, but certainly evidence of a Victorian gentleman who enjoyed his sport and, moreover, was good at it. The *mens sana in corpore sano* ethic and spirit of muscular Christianity prevailed as the Mayor quoted Lord Lytton:

> Better than fame is still the wish for fame,
> The constant training for a glorious strife;
> The athlete nurtured for the Olympian games
> Gains strength at least for life.

On the football, however, there is strong evidence that he was an extremely effective full-back and centre-half (his height of just under 6 feet and muscular frame of more than 14 stones would equip him ideally for the role), representing the Priory Football Club for more than a decade and ceasing to play the game only on his marriage in 1885.

In the 1870s, Reigate Priory, many of its members cricketers switching sports for the winter (but that's how Sheffield Wednesday and Derby County started), was one of the leading clubs and one of the fifteen participants in the very first FA Cup competition in 1871/72. However, that distinction is somewhat diluted by the fact that they withdrew from their first round tie against Royal Engineers allowing their opponents a walk-over and an eventual passage to the Final. No professionalism then of course (at least officially); that was to come in the next decade when clubs like Aston Villa, Blackburn Rovers, Preston North End and West Bromwich Albion were to eclipse the amateur ethos of public-school based sides, but until that time came, Reigate managed to have a share in what limited limelight football enjoyed. Their record in the FA Cup was not particularly distinguished. Only once in 1875/76 did they progress beyond the first round, only to be beaten 8-0 by Cambridge University in the second. They were founder members of the Surrey Football Association and did rather better in the local Surrey Senior Cup, contesting all five of the finals between 1882/83 and 1886/87 and winning two of them.

In the early stages, it was all very casual and informal. The football club was formed in 1870, only seven years after the

---

47   *Reigate, Redhill, Dorking and Epsom Journal* 10 24 June 1879

establishment of the Football Association, but before the secession of Blackheath and before Laws were uniform throughout the game. An early match against Redhill in early 1871 in which James Nightingale, Cricket Club secretary, played for Reigate brought the following observations.

> As the rules of this club do not tally with those in the neighbourhood, and consequently there is a difficulty in making matches, it has therefore been arranged that at a general meeting of members on Friday evening next the Rules should be revised.[48]

Later in the year in a match against Crystal Palace (not the present Football League Club) only seven of the Reigate Club put in an appearance, the other four, said the local newspaper,[49] being too delicate to send word that they were unable to venture out. Crystal Palace found three substitutes for the Reigate team and the match went ahead. Organisation was to improve in later years and Read would play a part in that.

In 1875, the only occasion Reigate actually won an FA Cup tie, Read played an important part, as his team hung on to a lead by a single goal.

> Some dangerous onslaughts were made on the Reigate goal, but owing to the brilliant back play of Laker and Read, assisted by the excellent goal-keeping of Sargant, their attempts were frustrated and no further result obtained.[50]

Throughout his twenties, except when injured and on overseas cricket tours, Walter was a regular and important member of the team, demonstrating his versatility when used as an emergency forward.

Reigate Priory v East Grinstead

> This return match was played at Reigate on Saturday last resulting in a victory for the home side by three goals to none. Notwithstanding the inclement state of the weather and slippery nature of the ground, some excellent play was shown by both sides. For Reigate Read displayed splendid form forward, two goals being placed to his credit, the third being kicked by Smith.[51]

---

48   *Reigate, Redhill, Dorking and Epsom Journal* 31 January 1871
49   *Reigate, Redhill, Dorking and Epsom Journal* 26 December 1871
50   *Surrey Mirror* 2 November 1875
51   *Reigate, Redhill, Dorking and Epsom Journal* 30 January 1877

In early 1884 with the game growing in popularity and local support increasing accordingly, Reigate beat Royal Engineers 1-0 in a second round Surrey Cup match. It was

> played in beautiful weather, and in the presence of a large number of spectators, who had apparently come from all parts to witness the game, whilst another gratifying feature was the presence on the ground of many of the members of the families in the neighbourhood.

> Hobbs and F Burtenshaw among the backs and Read (who during the second part of the game took a place in the centre) played in their usual reliable and effective manner.[52]

He was also instrumental in organising matches

> On Wednesday next a football match between an eleven selected by Mr W.W. Read and the Lennox Club. The following are down to play for Mr W.W. Read...[53]

and his absence through injury was a major reason for Reigate's failure to retain the trophy which they had won in its inaugural season.

> This fine football player, who has proved such a strength to the Reigate team this season unfortunately met with an accident in the match v Barnes. Every one will regret this, and at the same time heartily wish that his inconvenience will be but of a temporary character only and that he will soon be able to take his old place at back, where he has on more than one occasion saved his team from defeat.[54]

He was unable to take part in the semi-final against Dorking at the neutral venue of Guildford which Reigate won 2-1 and the *Surrey Mirror* expressed the view that their chance of retaining was dependent on Read's being fit to play.

> The final tie between Reigate Priory and Barnes will be played at Kennington Oval today (Sat). Both Clubs can present an exceedingly good record for the season, Barnes having suffered defeat on only two occasions. Reigate has been defeated also on two occasions. We think the match will probably depend on the ability of W W Read to represent Reigate. Should he be well enough to perform, we shall expect to see Reigate victorious,

---

52   *Sunday Mirror* 19 January 1884
53   *Surrey Mirror* 26 January 1884
54   *Surrey Mirror* 9 February 1884

otherwise Barnes will just manage to defeat the holders of the cup.[55]

In the event, Read did not play 'in consequence of an injury received on a previous occasion prevented the famous Surrey cricketer from taking part in the game whatsoever.'[56]

Despite his subsequent domestic and international cricket commitments, his interest in football continued and in 1892 he became Honorary Secretary of the Surrey County Football Association.[57]

Reigate Priory Cricket Club is immensely proud of Walter Read's association with it and continues to be a successful club, at the time of writing (2011) having won the Surrey Championship for four of the last seven years and boasting current and former Surrey players, Chris Murtagh, Jason Roy and Simon and Daryl King.

55   *Surrey Mirror* 15 March 1884
56   *Surrey Mirror* 22 March 1884
57   *Scores and Biographies* Vol XIV p xcv

Chapter Three
Surrey 1873/80

Although Read was and remained through his career an 'amateur' (but more of that later), he did not have the advantages of public school pitches and coaching that were enjoyed by those from whose social class he had no wish to disassociate himself. He was essentially self-taught with a natural eye for a ball.

He was recommended to the county by Henry Jupp, but because of his commitments at his father's school was able to represent Surrey only in the vacations, until that all changed with his appointment to the post (some might say 'sinecure') of Assistant Secretary to C.W.Alcock.

He made his début for Surrey against Yorkshire at the Oval on 11 August 1873 at the age of 17 years 261 days and is described in *Wisden* as 'W.Read, Esq. (Colt)'.[58] At the time he was the youngest ever to have played first-class cricket for the county and in the intervening years there have been only ten younger. *Scores and Biographies* gives him a brief biography up to 1877 at this point, judging him to be 'a sound and free hitter, bidding fair if he continues the game to arrive at the top of the tree'. His education and club cricket are erroneously conflated into 'Reigate Priory School' and it is mentioned that he has not yet appeared at Lord's.[59] Playing on that ground was a criterion (though not an exclusive one) for an entry in *Scores and Biographies*, however insignificant the fixture, and it appears retrospectively bizarre that not having played there is worthy of mention. He had after all by this time played almost a couple of dozen first-class matches on other grounds and was not in fact to appear on the St John's Wood ground before 1881 when he was able to devote himself full-time to first-class cricket.

He made 3 and 14 against Yorkshire, following it up against Kent the following week with 0 and 39, the highest score of the Surrey second innings, but he had had a taste of the milieu which was to

---

58   *Wisden* 1874 p 119
59   *Scores and Biographies* Vol XII pp 894-895

be his natural environment for the next quarter of a century.

The local press reported that the new Surrey gentleman – W Reed [sic] was not a free bat but had a good defence and kept wicket tolerably well.[60]

Two years later he topped the county's batting averages. Still aged only 20, in 1876, he scored his maiden first-class century, 106, against Kent at Maidstone.

In the return match at the Oval, he captained the side. Aged 20 years 275 days at the time, he is the third youngest captain in the county's history. His opposite number was Lord Harris, himself appointed captain of his county at a similar age. Now in his sixth year of leadership, he was to exert a huge influence on the game, defending, nay promoting, the amateur ethos and throughout his life, keeping professionals in their place and finding the concept of a professional as captain utterly abhorrent. His blood pressure remained normal, however, as Surrey stuck to a tradition that was to obtain for almost another century. Notwithstanding the presence of several experienced professionals, the youthful Read was appointed as captain for the match in the absence of regular captain Allen Chandler who replaced George Strachan for just one season.

On this occasion, however, the younger man's team came out on top. It was, as they say, a good toss to lose. Kent chose to bat and soon found themselves back in the hutch (or two hutches, presumably, one for Lord Harris and the other Kent amateurs and one for the professionals) for 66, George Jones cleaning up with 6 for 10. Although Read's own contribution was insignificant, his team built a substantial first innings lead and despite Kent coming back in the second dig, it was insufficient to prevent a 10-wicket win for the home side and a 100% record for the county's stand-in captain. He was never appointed official captain, however, playing for most of his career under John Shuter and then Kingsmill Key.

A score of 60 not out against Yorkshire on a difficult wicket at The Oval in 1876 had demonstrated for the first of many times in his career that he was far from being merely a flat-track bully and could perform on bad wickets too. It followed 94 and 41 in the tied match against Middlesex

> Mr Read went to wickets with the score at 18 for two down; he was 9th man out, 196 runs having been made while he was

---

60   *Reigate, Redhill, Dorking and Epsom Journal* 19 August 1873

playing his patient and excellent 94, which included a superb drive for 6 from Flanagan, five 4's, six 3's and 28 singles.[61]

The following year, 1877, he was selected by W.G.Grace for the Gentlemen-Players match at Prince's and distinguished himself with 72, an innings described by *Cricket* as 'brilliant'[62] and drawing the comment from *Wisden* that 'this was Mr Read's first Gentlemen and Players match; it is to be hoped it will not be his last for the cricket he played was good enough for any match.'[63]

His highest score to date followed shortly afterwards, 140 against Yorkshire at The Oval in an opening partnership of 206 with his mentor, Henry Jupp.

> Mr W.W. Read and Jupp making 206 runs before the first Surrey wicket fell, and ten of the Eleven Yorkshiremen taking a bowling turn in that innings, mark this as the most remarkable of the many interesting matches played on the Oval in 1877.[64]

In its report on Surrey the following year, *Wisden* underlined his value to the side

> the Committee would be wanting in gratitude were they not to make mention of the very valuable services rendered by Mr. W.W.Read during the year.[65]

In 1878, selected for an 'England' team which played intermittently against county sides, his batting was considered 'the best on the side'[66] and a major contributory factor to the defeat of Gloucestershire. Although his commitments at his father's school prevented his playing regularly, except in the holidays, he continued to impress in the following seasons, in particular with a 93 at Cheltenham in 1880 and, in 1881, his highest to date, 160 against Kent, 'for hard driving and well-timed hitting one of the best innings we have ever seen.'[67]

---

61   *Wisden* 1877 p 160 but CricketArchive shows that he was 8th man out,
62   19 April 1883
63   *Wisden* 1878 p 27
64   *Wisden* 1878 p 150
65   *Wisden* 1878 p 131
66   *Cricket* 19 April 1883
67   *Cricket* 19 April 1883

Chapter Four
Assistant Secretary... You're 'aving a larf

The role of Assistant Secretary was a fig-leaf covering the reality of a highly paid professional. Unsurprisingly, the arrangement was not without its critics and detractors, both from the cricket writers of the day and the professionals alongside whom Read played. Rev R.S. Holmes in a feature quoted almost a hundred years later by David Kynaston in his book on Bobby Abel wrote –

> One county pays an amateur a salary of £250 for playing cricket, though this sum is ostensibly given him for the discharge of official duties, which he no more fulfils than I do. Expenses are also allowed, and of the most liberal order, besides a free pass between his home and the county ground. Say what we will, he is simply the best-paid professional in his county, though he comes out of the central gate of the pavilion, and gets an occasional touch of the cap from the professionals.

Kynaston goes on to say that Holmes was almost certainly referring to Read whose original salary was £120 which, in 1883, was raised to £150. On top of this was a season ticket from Reigate to London and from 1886 onwards he also received an autumn honorarium of £100. Later he was given a match fee of four guineas. Kynaston also points out that, according to *The Athletic News* he received £1317 10s for going to Australia in 1887/88.[68]

1881 was a significant year in Read's career. He accepted the post of Assistant Secretary to Charles Alcock, a device to allow him to devote the whole of the summer to playing cricket for Surrey and representative sides for which he might be selected. There was nothing secretive about the arrangement. Like his contemporary W.G.Grace, he became a professional cricketer masquerading as an amateur. Unlike many of his amateur colleagues from a public school and/or university environment, supplemented by inherited wealth, he was from a family and financial circumstances

---

68   Kynaston *Bobby Abel, Professional Batsman* pp130-131

which, though associated with a highly respected profession, did not allow him to play cricket as a full-time occupation for out-of-pocket expenses only. Conversely, he did not share the working-class origins of his professional colleagues. Social class was significant in Victorian society, but like the diluted version of it a century and a half later, did not correlate directly with wealth. Like Grace, Read could not afford financially to be an amateur, nor did he wish socially to be a professional. The solution was simple. He became a paid amateur, drawing a salary and expenses from a job he did not do (or at least made no pretence of doing full time – certainly not in the summer) to recompense him for one that he did.

He was an educated man, literate and articulate and had been Joint Secretary of the Reigate Priory, so he was not without the skills required for the job, but it is clear that he did not spend much time using them. There is some evidence that he did some, but not much, work as Assistant Secretary. A set of committee minutes is in his handwriting[69] and there is the occasional list of new members written into minute books.[70] Furthermore, he represented the club on occasion, along with the Secretary and the Captain at the annual meeting of county secretaries, so although it would not be true to say that he did absolutely nothing as Assistant Secretary, it cannot be pretended that the appointment was anything other than an ingenious device to enable a not-so-well-off amateur to play full-time professional cricket. It was to be imitated by other clubs and continued well into the following century. For instance immediately after the Second World War A.D.G Matthews was Assistant Secretary at Glamorgan, Desmond Eager Joint Secretary for Hampshire and 'Billy' Griffith Captain and Secretary at Sussex; later Trevor Bailey became Secretary at Essex.

E.V.B Christian wrote, perhaps idealistically, in *Cricket* that cricketers have long been accustomed to boast that their sport levels ranks,

> The Earl, the Marquis and the Dook,
> The Groom, the Butler and the Cook,
> They all shall equal be.[71]

That may have been true on the field and Trevelyan may well have

---

69   18 April 1889
70   17 April 1890 and 7 May 1891
71   *Cricket* 17 September 1891

been correct when he said that had the French aristocracy played cricket with their peasants there would have been no French Revolution, but off the field the social divisions of Victorian England seemed set in stone, and social mobility, though far from impossible, was less likely than it was subsequently to become in the following century.

It is, however, difficult to contradict Major Wardill's level-headed analysis twenty years later of the amateur-professional divide and the hypocrisy involved in maintaining English social class distinctions.

> There has been much discussion in the press of late years about the payments made to professionals and amateurs – much of the discussion being very wide of the mark – that the following pronouncements by Major Wardill to a representative of the *Evening News* are of interest:
>
> He could not understand why the Australians were regarded in some quarters as professionals. We have no great leisured class in the Colonies as you have here, and in order that the best men may come to England, it is necessary to conduct each tour strictly on business lines. Should profits accrue after defraying expenses they are divided equally among the members of the team to recoup them for their loss of time and salary during their eight months' absence.
>
> If you call the Australians professionals, Major Wardill continued with a smile, then the English amateurs who come to the colonies are even more so. Take the last team for instance. The Melbourne C C paid for everything – steamer passages, rail and hotel expenses, tips etc. In addition, each man received a sum running into three figures as pin-money. And, indeed in the case of one of the amateurs, the Melbourne CC was debited with the cost of the outfit he bought before embarking.[72]

Not quite on the scale of the scandal over the expenses of Members of Parliament which was to hit the U K in 2009 with its ramifications into duck-houses and the 'flipping' of second homes, but very much in the same vein and sufficient to suggest that the line between the amateur and the professional was blurred and had less to do with money than with class distinctions.

On the whole, however, the Assistant Secretary ruse was entirely

---

72   *Cricket* 1 May 1902

successful to the extent it allowed Read to concentrate full time on his cricket and be in all but name a professional. Having been prevented by his school duties, he now was a regular feature of the matches. He was invited for the first time since then to play for the Gentlemen against the Players in 1882, making 21 and 5 in a match won by the professionals by 87 runs, their first victory at the Oval in this long-standing fixture since 1865 – a result seen in some quarters as being symptomatic of a shift in the balance of power.

Amateur cricket is beginning to suffer appreciably. It remains to be seen how correct our estimate is, but at the present time it seems as if the relative positions enjoyed by the Amateur and Professional traditions are about to undergo a change.[73]

Assistant Secretary and cricketer - as seen by
The Cricket Field's *cartoonist at the time of Read's benefit in 1895.*

---

73   *Cricket* 6 July 1882

Chapter Five
Surrey and England 1881/87

1881

Reigate Priory's Annual Report for 1881 regretted the loss of Walter Read's services. But Reigate's loss was Surrey's gain.

In 1881, now for the first time able to play regularly,

> Mr W.W. Read was able to play in every match, and proved the mainstay of the Surrey batting, beside showing exceptional form as a wicket-keeper. His brilliant hitting in the fifteen matches in which he took part, place him at the head of all three important batting columns. (total runs, largest innings and average)[74]

Against Notts at The Oval,

> Mr Pontifex played brilliantly for 89; a 5, nine 4's, six 3's and six 2's being his principal hits. Mr Read's 63 was even a more brilliant performance, his hits taking this extraordinary form: fourteen 4's, one 3, one 2,and two singles.[75]

His highest score of the season, 160 against Kent at Maidstone, while not flawless, was clearly entertaining,

> Mr W W Read gave three chances while scoring his 160, but it was nevertheless a grand innings, and the severity of his hitting may be judged from the composition of his score – three 6's, twenty-nine 4's (134 in 32 hits), four 2's, and eighteen singles.[76]

1882

For the second season, as would be the case for the remainder of his career, he had the opportunity to play almost every day of the summer (or at least, six days a week, the Victorian sabbath prohibiting entertainment of any thoughts of Sunday sport) and

---

74   *Wisden* 1882 p 166
75   *Wisden* 1882 p 175
76   *Wisden* 1882 p 197

began the season with a 94 for Reigate District against Surrey Colts. Later – and we are still, of course, in pre-declaration days – he had 263 out of a total of 557 for Reigate Priory against Guildford, on the way sharing in a partnership of 368 for the third wicket.

The match was followed by Gentlemen of England v Australia at The Oval, so it was a useful elongated net. He made 17 and 19 in a match which the tourists won by an innings and one run. Nowadays, he would more likely have prepared by 'resting'. However, his performances for Surrey were by the standards he had set in earlier years a little disappointing, and, although *Cricket* was complimentary about his century against Kent at The Oval – he 'hit very freely, and his 117 was got without a mistake. His success was the more popular, as he had recently been a little out of luck –, the end of the season...'[77]

The end-of-season conclusion was that 'Mr W.W. Read played a very fine innings against Kent but he hardly came up to expectations formed at the outset.'[78]

WG and WW.
[Roger Mann Collection]

77   *Cricket* 3 August 1882
78   *Cricket* 14 September 1882

Once again, Read had led Surrey's batting, albeit with a lower average than the previous year. It was not his greatest season, 882 runs at 25.94.

> In batting Mr. W W Read again played in all the matches, and again appears at the head of the list in all three important columns, but not with so good an average as in the previous year.[79]

1883

Read's form in Australia continued into the domestic season of 1883 as he moved seamlessly between international and club cricket, his 145 for Reigate Priory against Incogniti being preceded by 168 for Surrey against Hampshire on a re-laid and apparently batsman-friendly pitch at The Oval when the home side, at one stage scoring 300+ in three hours, reached 650, at the time the highest team total in first-class cricket in England. He led the first-class averages for most of the season and ended with 1573 runs at 47.66

Demonstrating his all-round versatility and his above-average competence as a wicket-keeper, he stepped into the breach against Leicestershire at Grace Road in May. Already captain of the side, he had a stumping and scored the only half- century of the match, but Surrey still lost a low scoring encounter by seven runs.

The 1884 Test Matches

1884 for Surrey and Read was a modest season for both Surrey and its Assistant Secretary. It was in international cricket that season that he was to make his most memorable contribution.

In looking ahead to the international season, *Cricket* could not avoid also looking back to events two years earlier.

> A reference to the discreditable defeat of the picked Eleven of England at The Oval in 1882 will convince any lover of sport of what our humiliation would be should Australia inflict on us a repetition of the disaster of two years ago.[80]

Anglo-Australian Test Matches at The Oval (formerly the Kennington Oval and in more recent times, the Foster's Oval, AMP Oval, Brit Oval, Kia Oval or whatever sponsor happens to be

79   *Wisden* 1883 p 115
80   *Cricket* 27 March 1884

passing through) have a habit of becoming part of cricket folklore. The contests of 2005 and 2009 saw the Ashes return to England, as did that of 1953, while 1948 witnessed Bradman's farewell Test Match. 'Where the Ashes were won' was a Marketing Department -coined slogan which briefly adorned Surrey stationery for a few months in the mid-decade Pietersen-mania days, only to be quietly dropped as the euphoria subsided with a 5-0 defeat in the Antipodes eighteen months later. 'Where the Ashes were born' might have been less transient for it was here that England's first defeat on English soil in 1882 gave rise to the mock obituary in the *Sporting Times* and the concept of 'The Ashes'. Two years before that, Charles Alcock had launched Test cricket in England and two years after that, the Test match of 1884 was memorable, if for different reasons.

It was the third match of a series of three, the convention of The Oval hosting the final Test of the summer being early established. There had been a draw at Old Trafford and England had an easy win by an innings and five runs at Lord's. Before the establishment of the Board of Control of 'Test' Matches at Home in 1899, the responsibility for team selection lay with the host venue and inevitably there was a degree of bias and favouritism. Read, though having not had a bad season for Surrey and eventually again topping the averages for the season, did not play at Manchester and contributed a modest eleven and seven to the win at the other London venue. He was included in the team for the match at The Oval which began on Monday 11 August.

W.L. Murdoch made test cricket's first double century as Australia accumulated 551 in an innings unique in Test match annals in that all eleven of the fielding side had a turn with the ball, including WW with seven overs of his slow lobs. Unlike wicketkeeper Lyttelton who had 4 for 19, he had no success.

At 181 for 8, England were well on the way to following on and an innings defeat. WW, batting at No.10, had other ideas. He failed to avert the follow-on, but with what he later said was his best innings of 117, ensured that defeat was avoided. He reached his century in 36 scoring strokes and in all, his innings lasted 120 minutes (155 balls). It remains the highest score by a no 10 in Test cricket, a fairly meaningless record, as it is bizarre that he should be batting there in the first place. Exactly why one selected for his batting rather than his slow lobs was batting at no 10 is a matter for conjecture.

One version is that, feeling himself to be out of form, he asked to be put down the order. That may be the 'establishment' spin, but it looks hardly likely.

> Mr. Read had been rather out of form before the match commenced, and had for this reason insisted, when the batting order was being drawn up, that he was not entitled to occupy a higher position than No.10.[81]

If he were so out of form it is unlikely that he would have been selected in the first place and his record coming in to the match, while not brilliant, was hardly indicative of one who was out of form. Since the Lord's Test, he had had 21 against Yorkshire, 43 and 29 against Nottinghamshire and his sole single figure innings of nine against Kent was top score in a total of 44 all out.[82]

The more likely version is that he had had words with captain Lord Harris earlier, aristocracy and autocracy had prevailed and he had been demoted,'...ostensibly he had had a row with Harris and had been relegated in the hope that he would cool down.'[83]

It is recalled in one of his Obituaries as 'the innings of his life'.

> England had a magnificent eleven and Mr Read, though he ought to have gone in earlier was tenth in the batting order. In ordinary circumstances he would not have had much chance of distinction, but Scotton who had gone in first and was firmly set, kept up such an impressive defence that the tenth [sic] wicket added over 150 runs...the way in which Mr Read punished the bowling of Spofforth, Palmer, Giffen and Boyle will never be forgotten by those fortunate enough to be present. His innings ranks among the finest ever played in Test matches, and after the lapse of 22 years it is still talked about.[84]

More than a hundred years later, Gerry Cotter sees the innings in the context of Read's sometimes choleric temperament. 'His character is epitomized by his famous innings at the Oval in 1884 when he struck 117 furious (and match-saving) runs because he was annoyed with Lord Harris at being left until number ten.'[85]

81   F S Ashley-Cooper in *Surrey Cricket: its History and Associations* p 375
82   What goes around comes around. Read was bowled by Frank Lipscomb whose father he had defied on his début for Reigate Priory in 1868. Lipscomb jr's 5-19 were his best figures in first-class cricket.
83   Coldham *Lord Harris* p 60
84   *Surrey Mirror* 11 January 1907
85   *The Ashes Captains* p 41

Read himself throws no light on his state of mind. In his review of the season in his *Annals of Cricket*, having mentioned W.G.Grace's three centuries against the Australians, he blandly records: 'I made a good show for England at the Oval. Going in tenth, I scored 117 runs in under two hours. My partner, Scotton, going in first, scored 90.'[86]

Whatever the reason, it seems that the innings was played in something of a red mist and remained memorable both for the batsman and the spectators.

He had an ideal foil in William Scotton, the Nottinghamshire blocker supreme, forerunner of Bailey, Boycott and Tavaré, who had opened with Grace and was still there at the fall of the eighth wicket. Scotton's first 50 (214 balls) remains one of the half dozen slowest for England and the ninth wicket partnership of 151 is still the highest for England against Australia – the only such partnership record to survive from the nineteenth century .

Cricket summarised the partnership as follows.

> The chief features were the extraordinary defence of Scotton and the brilliant hitting of Mr W W Read. Scotton went in first and was ninth out with the total at 332. He was batting altogether for five hours and three quarters and his patience was invaluable to his side. He never made a mistake that we saw, and his innings was for defensive cricket in every way extraordinary – a performance of which he has thoroughly good reason to be proud. Mr Read's 117 was as remarkable, though in quite a different style. He played all the Australian bowling with the greatest confidence, and his batting was distinctly the feature of the innings. He was only in two-hours-and-a quarter and everyone will be pleased that he so completely justified his place in the representative eleven of England by such a masterly display of batting.[87]

Eighteen years later, in one of W.A. Bettesworth's *Chats on the Cricket Field*, Fred Boyington, the long-serving Surrey scorer, at the time in his first year on the circuit, recalling the heat and large crowd, identifies the match by Read's innings.

> One of the most trying times I have had was in the match at the Oval in 1884 between England and Australia – the match in which Mr Walter Read played such a grand innings, going in,

---

86   p 173
87   14 August 1884

Cricket Match played at The Oval between England and England

Order of going in	Name of the Batsman	England — First Innings — Figures on scored	How Out	Bowler's Name	Runs
1	W.G. Grace	141112144	run	D.M—	19
2	Scotton	1441 / 4121113311214111424213412	C. Scott	Giffen	90
3	Barnes	12411424121	C. McDonnell	Spofforth	19
4	Shrewsbury	1414	C. Blackham	McDonnell	10
5	A.G. Steel	4111433211121114	L.B.W	Palmer	31
6	Ulyett	1118211	C. Bannerman	Palmer	10
7	Barlow	0	C. Murdoch	Palmer	0
8	Lord Harris	21434	L.B.W	Palmer	14
9	Hon A Lyttelton	111112 / 2141422132112424441124	Bowled	Spofforth	8
10	W.W. Read	421444424424424	Bowled	Boyle	114
11	Peate	4	not out		4
	Byes	4			4
	Leg Byes				8
	Wide Balls				6
	No Balls				
			Total of First Innings		346

Runs at the fall of each Wicket	1st=32	2nd=60	3rd=75	4th=120	5th=136	6th=136	7th=160	8th=181	9th=333	10th=346

*Read's Test match century v Australia at The Oval in 1884 -
extract from the official scorebook.
[Surrey County Cricket Club]*

I think, at the fall of the ninth wicket[88], making 117 without a blemish and no doubt saving the match for England.[89]

B J Wakley's *Classic Centuries*[90] shows that Read made only one mistake when Spofforth dropped a hard return catch and that it took him 113 minutes to reach his century, having overtaken Scotton (then on 84) eight minutes previously.

1885

After a winter off (maybe he did a bit of work as Assistant Secretary), he began the 1885 season in fine style, scoring runs in club and Club and Ground matches, before recording a century against Essex in a two-day non first-class county match.

> Mr W.W.READ has already in a County match fully justified my prediction that he was likely to be in rare run-getting form for Surrey this season. Considering that it was his first chance in an important fixture and that the ground was not quite recovered from recent rains, his performance at the Oval on Monday in scoring 143 out of 205 while he was in, must be accounted as remarkable. Though one of the daily sporting papers thought right to speak disparagingly of it as a whole, it will be enough for ordinary judges to learn that he gave no chance until he had scored 115.[91]

In a useful warm-up for the first-class season, Surrey won by an innings and 48 runs. There were many such innings, many such reports, particularly in this and the two subsequent seasons as Read, now about to enter his fourth decade, reaches a plateau marking the highest point of his career. It would be tedious to record them all, but almost without exception, all are complimentary, and reflect a more than competent *de jure* amateur, but *de facto* professional.

A double century in an innings victory over Essex at Leyton preceded what was perhaps his outstanding innings that summer. There was also a match-saving 159 in the follow-on for the Gentlemen against the Players at The Oval. With some help from Scotton, the joint hero of the Test match on the same ground the previous season, but now an opponent, he batted long enough to avoid a second collapse and obviate an innings defeat. It

---

88   actually, the eighth
89   18 December 1902
90   *Classic Centuries* p 22
91   *Cricket* 14 May 1885

was his only century in 23 appearances in what was at the time considered a prestigious fixture, though he did have eight other scores of over fifty. Noting that Mr W.G.Grace, Mr W.W.Read and Gunn all played up to their reputations - again bracketed with distinguished company – *Cricket* reported on the third day's play,

> Mr Read, who was not out 66 on Friday night continued to play grand cricket on Saturday until he had made 125 when he was missed in the field by Scotton. This was a fatal mistake by the Players and one which materially influenced the result. Mr Read added 34 runs when he was caught at short slip off the wicket-keeper, thus bringing to an end one of the finest innings ever recorded for the Gentlemen. Going in second wicket down at 13 he was seventh out at 306, having been batting for four hours and three-quarters. With the exception of the very hard return to Peate and his chance late in the innings to Scotton, his play was without a fault. His figures were twenty-four fours, six threes, ten twos and twenty-five singles.[92]

National averages in *Cricket* in early August, though including matches not subsequently considered first-class, show Read in the lead with 53.31 (1727 from 32 completed innings) some distance ahead of Gunn in second place with 38.21 (1199 from 31).[93] He did not remain there but ended the season with a respectable enough first-class average of 44.76 from 42 innings.[94]

1886

Among Read's more significant contributions that year was his 94 in The Oval Test Match, this time batting more appropriately at No.4, rather than No.10; as he had in the previous series, he narrowly missed out on consecutive Test centuries on his home ground. He had already been England's top scorer in the four wicket win at Old Trafford and, though playing a less significant individual role, was part of a team that took an unbeatable 2-0 lead in the three-match series with a comfortable innings victory at Lord's. At The Oval,

> When it seemed almost certain that Mr. Read would reach his 100 he was out to a well-judged catch in the long field. Out

---

92   *Cricket* 9 July 1885
93   *Cricket* 6 August 1885. .31 and .21 are not decimal fractions, but the 'number over', reflecting the usual practice at the time.
94   Cricket Archive – and a genuine decimal fraction this time.

of 202 runs scored while he was at the wickets, he made 94 by perfect cricket. He hardly gave a fair chance, and seldom seemed in the least difficulty with the bowling. He was batting for about three hours and a half and hit eight 4's two 3's and fifteen 2's.[95]

England went on to win the match by an innings and 217 runs, Australia finding no answer to Lohmann and Briggs. As in 1884, Scotton had demonstrated his ability to 'bat time'. He shared an opening partnership of 170 with Grace to which his contribution was 34 in 3 ¾ hours, including a period of 67 minutes when he failed to score at all. It was Scotton who was the inspiration behind *Punch*'s parody of Tennyson.

THE WAIL OF THE WEARY

Block, block, block
At the foot of thy wicket, O Scotton!
And I would that my tongue could utter
My boredom. You *won't* put the pot on!

O nice for the bowler, my boy,
That each ball like a barn-door, you play;
O, nice for yourself, I suppose,
That you stick at the wickets all day.

And the clock's slow hands go on,
And you still keep up your sticks;
But oh for the lift of a smiting hand,
And the sound of a swipe for six!

Block, block, block
At the foot of thy wickets, oh do!
But one hour of Grace or Walter Read
Were worth a week of you.[96]

So, in his time Read became iconic in the sense of being symbolic of something greater, rather than in the twenty-first century sense when everything from an Olympic stadium to a plastic duck has become iconic.

Sadly, Scotton was to take his own life in 1893 at the age of 37, but the bracketing of Grace and Read is significant, as is their pairing, batting against Australia in the painting by G.H.Barrable and R.Ponsonby Staples of an imaginary match at Lord's attended

---

95   *Wisden* 1887 p 47
96   *Cricket* 26 July 1886

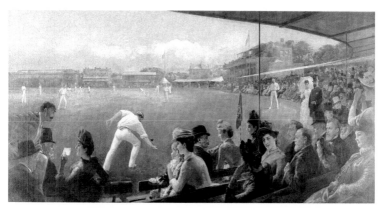

*Grace and Read batting against Australia in the painting by G.H.Barrable
and R.Ponsonby Staples of an imaginary match at Lord's attended inter alios
by the Prince of Wales, Princess Alexandra and Lily Langtree.*

*[MCC, Bridgeman Art Library and the executors of the estate
of the late Hazel Radcliffe-Dolling].*

inter alios by the Prince of Wales, Princess Alexandra and Lily
Langtree. The following extract from *Cricket*'s jocular advice to a
school captain suggests that Read and in this case Shrewsbury are
clearly benchmarks or rôle models for the younger generation.

> You will find that an acquaintance with old cricketing authors
> will not be unserviceable. e g if your point refuses to stand less
> than 12 or 14 yards from the wicket because W W Read and
> Shrewsbury do not, you may, with effect, remind (or inform)
> him that Nyren states the proper distance to be 3 yards.[97]

He was also bracketed with W G in a piece in *Cricket*, 'The
Influence of Cricket on the Lives of Men' which oozes with
Victorian sanctimoniousness.

> Oh! that first century. Can W G remember his? or Walter Read
> his? perhaps not, lost among the multitude; but still I fancy
> they can.[98]

There can be no serious doubt about W.G.Grace's supremacy as a
batsman in the nineteenth century. Whatever may be said about
his intimidation of umpires and his gamesmanship, his record of
first-class cricket spanning five decades remains unchallenged
and unchallengeable. Yet there were times in the 80s when in
statistical terms at any rate Read certainly ran him close and

---

97   *Cricket* 26 January 1893
98   *Cricket* 25 November 1886

seemed to be in better form than 'the Champion'.

Meanwhile, away from the Test arena, Read continued to show outstanding form for Surrey, finishing the season with 1825 first-class runs at an average of 42.44. He showed outstanding form in an innings victory over Leicestershire, not at the time first-class.

> ...the feature of the innings was the brilliant cricket of Mr W W Read. In three hours and a quarter he made 157 runs without a mistake, carrying out his bat after one of the best displays of batting he has ever given. He has not this season been seen to better advantage and his hitting towards the close was very clean and hard.[99]

and the purple patch continued in an end-of season match at Hove for the South of England against the tourists.

> He was at the wickets two hours and forty minutes, and in this time, scored 102 not out, this being his highest innings hit against the Australians during the summer. His play all-round was admirable, his off drives being very hard and clean and his cuts well-timed, while his leg hits caused frequent applause.[100]

In December, in a rare commitment to the duties of his post as Assistant Secretary, he accompanied Fred Burbidge and C.W. Alcock to the Annual Meeting of County Secretaries.

1887

For the third consecutive season, Read had a first-class batting average of over 40, these days a benchmark for a competent county batsman, but in the late nineteenth century some way above the norm. Now verging on the prodigious, he recorded the achievement, at the time unique, of double centuries in consecutive innings.

Firstly, against Lancashire at Old Trafford in a match which Surrey won by an innings and 134 runs –

> The feature of the Surrey batting...was the remarkable stand by Messrs Read and Roller on the second day. Mr Read joined Mr Roller who had been not out over night at eight minutes past twelve on Friday, and it was just six o'clock before the latter was caught at the wicket, their partnership which had

---

99 *Cricket* 2 September 1886
100 *Wisden* 1887 p 60

The Surrey team of 1887
[Surrey County Cricket Club]

extended over four hours, resulting in an addition of 305 runs to the score...the only mistake in Read's fine innings of 247 – the highest he has made for the county – being a chance in the long field at 82.[101]

Then, he came within three of that score against Cambridge University at The Oval the following week, on Jubilee Day before he ran out of partners in yet another innings victory.

His innings was not finished until the total had been raised to 543 of which number W W Read, who carried out his bat contributed no less than 244. This performance was a more remarkable one following as it did his score of 247 at Manchester last Friday, and we believe two successive innings of over two hundred in important matches are without parallel. He was batting altogether five hours and twenty minutes and with the exception of one chance when he had made 186 there was no mistake in an extraordinary display of cricket.[102]

Wisden, however, is slightly less complimentary, suggesting that

101   *Cricket* 23 June 1887
102   *Cricket* 23 June 1887

there was something of a 'flat track bully' approach to some modest university bowling,

> ...the great feature of the day was the hitting of Mr W W Read who, at the drawing of stumps was not out 200.

> On the Tuesday (Jubilee Day) the game was continued and an immense crowd of people visited Kennington Oval, about 11,000 paying for admission at the turnstiles. Mr W W Read took out his bat for 244 and there is no saying how many he might have made had there been partners to stop with him. He has on occasion played finer cricket, but the moderate quality of the University bowling on a good wicket tempted him to play a risky game. On the whole, however, his display was an extraordinarily fine one, and he scarcely made a mistake except when, with his score at 137, he was nearly caught by Mr Buxton with one hand at third man.[103]

Earlier, he had been honoured with the captaincy of the England side which played MCC in the first match of the week which celebrated the centenary of what was at the time the premier club. His team won by an innings and 117 runs, centuries by Shrewsbury and Stoddart in an opening partnership of 266 and six for 62 from Lohmann ensuring that the hosts never really got a look in. Read himself took advantage of the platform established by the first wicket stand to make 74, showing 'fine, free cricket';[104] 'England' were just about at full strength. MCC probably regarded the whole week as a bit of a jolly. The next match in the 'week' was between a Veterans XI and the Gentlemen of MCC.

In 1890 Read became a member of the MCC,[105] playing twice for them against the Australians that summer, but he was never actively involved with 'the premier club' and his playing for them that season may not mean very much. He also played for Lord Sheffield's XI, Lord Londesborough's XI and the Lyric Club.

He made three other first-class centuries that summer of 1887 - against Derbyshire, Kent and Oxford University, and four other scores over 50. Bowlers win matches and Surrey became Champion County for the first time since 1864[106] largely because

---

103   *Wisden* 1888 p 7
104   *Cricket* 16 June 1887
105   *Scores and Biographies* Vol XIV p xcvi
106   However, as *Wisden* points out: 'The title of champion county is unreliable before 1890. In 1963 *Wisden* formally accepted the list of champions "most generally selected" by contemporaries as researched by the late Rowland Bowen.' This appears to be the most accurate available list but has no official status (*Wisden* 2011 p 369)

of the outstanding bowling of George Lohmann, but batsmen play their part and none played a larger one than Walter Read.

His performance on the second day of the Kent match impressed Albert Craig, the Surrey poet. Surrey were playing catch-up having conceded a first-innings lead of 120.

> When Mr Key joined Mr Read, each stood with bat in hand,
> They both struck out right manfully, both made a famous stand.
> They stood like British soldiers stand, they stood beside their guns,
> And in three hours, our favourites got two hundred well earned runs.

Read had 100, Key 179 and Craig's second day prediction was fulfilled on the third,

> Kent, good Old Kent, means victory, but it will not be so,
> If Surrey fail to win the match, 'twill finish in a draw.

On the social scene too he was becoming prominent:

> Mr WALTER READ, the well-known Surrey cricketer, is to take the chair at the smoking concert of the Forest Hill Club, to be held at the Bridge House Hotel tomorrow evening. The programme will include a flute solo by Mr C Spencer West the hon sec of the Club and a flautist very much above the average of amateurs, as well as a banjo solo by Professor Joe Daniels, who has often contributed to the amusement of cricketers on occasions of a similar kind.[107]

Already equipped with the required cricketing skills, Read was now developing the social skills required of a man chosen to captain England against MCC and, more significantly, in a Test match against Australia the following winter.

---

107   *Cricket* 19 May 1887

Chapter Six
Australia 1882/83 and 1887/88

Read's performances during the 1882 season, though not up to the standard of the previous season, were still sufficient for him to be invited to join the Hon Ivo Bligh on the seventh tour of Australia by an English team. Not until the twentieth century when touring teams were selected by and represented the MCC did such teams reflect the full strength of English cricket, being predominantly professional or predominantly amateur. This was the latter. In fact the original intention had been to take a team comprising solely Cambridge University men but there were issues of availability and other commitments, and eventually the nine amateurs (subsequently reduced to eight as Alfred Lucas withdrew for family reasons) were supplemented by four professionals taken along to do the bowling. That is an over-simplistic, but not entirely inaccurate analysis. Bligh's team has passed into cricketing folklore as being the first one to recapture 'The Ashes', though no one attached much significance to it at the time and history has embroidered the events on that tour with a significance they did not possess then.

From Read's point of view, the tour had more positives than negatives and was the forerunner of similarly successful ones (at least from a playing point of view) to Australia again and later to South Africa. He did not have the best of starts, however, a duck on the stopover in Colombo against a local Eighteen (comprised mainly of members of the garrison) being followed by five in a drawn match against South Australia, then playing on for one in the first first-class fixture of the tour against Victoria in Melbourne.

The matches are reported in detail in the *Sporting Life* and reproduced in *Cricket* under the anonymous authorship of *One of Them* – i e one of the team, identity unknown, but probably Read. In *Cricket's Burning Passion* Scyld Berry surmises that Read had the literacy and would have found the payment useful.

He does not confine himself to cricket reporting and adds a bit of colour by referring to the collision of the *Peshawar,* on which the team travelled, with a sailing ship after leaving Colombo. In his *Annals of Cricket*, the account is more detailed and personalised...

> our ship, the P. and O. *SS Peshawar*, came into collision with the *Glen Roy* barque, about 600 miles from Colombo. It was in that collision that Morley, the professional, had the misfortune to get one of his ribs broken, and which incapacitated him from playing regularly during the trip. It was altogether a terrible affair, and it is a wonder we were not all drowned. Two well-known players, whose faces generally carry the appearance of tanned leather, went as white as milk. One of them with a life-belt on was about to make for the water, when he saw sharks and stayed aboard. Two other popular professionals, who had not been on the best of terms, and as the prevailing idea was that we were "going down", one of them thought it would be as well that they should at least, "die friends" and approaching his brother professional, with a sigh, asked: "Don't you wish we were back at the old home?". "No, I don't, any more than you do, I'm done with you!" was the unexpected rejoinder. He evidently thinking their last moments had come.
>
> Beyond this unfortunate affair we had a very fine trip...[108]

He also comments on a visit to a goldmine, being entertained by the Mayor of Eaglehawk, banqueting with the previous summer's Australian tourists and, more significantly for the captain's future and cricket folklore, visiting Sir William Clarke at Sunbury on the outskirts of Melbourne. On Christmas Eve there may have more significance for the future of Anglo-Australian Test matches, but *Cricket* suggests there had been a previous visit there by the amateurs before the Victoria match in Melbourne.

> The amateur members of the team then proceeded to Sunbury to spend the Sunday with Sir W J Clarke of Rupertswood, who was one of the passengers on board the *Peshawar* with them. Leaving there on the following afternoon, they journeyed to Melbourne, where they were present at the banquet given to the Australian team who had just returned from England.[109]

Between the two trips to Sunbury, Read's form had begun to improve, 46 against New South Wales ('a good innings') being followed by 64 against Eighteen of Newcastle and District ('the

---

108   *Annals of Cricket* p 169-170
109   *Cricket* 16 February 1883

Surrey amateur was playing some very good cricket') and 55 against Eighteen of Ballarat where, as at Newcastle, he was the 'chief contributor'.

The story of 'The Ashes' has passed into cricket folklore – how after England's unexpected and humiliating defeat at The Oval in 1882 a mock obituary in the *Sporting Times* lamented the death of English cricket, the body of which would be cremated and the ashes taken to Australia. Those 'ashes' became tangible in the form of a terracotta urn presented to captain Ivo Bligh the following Christmas in Melbourne by his future wife, Florence Morphy. Not until Pelham Warner's tour of 1903/04 did the sporting icon become of public significance. Until then, The Ashes remained something of a private joke with occasional press references. Walter Read, however, along with several of his colleagues is immortalised in the Victorian doggerel that passes for an inscription on the urn, now played for every two years or so between England and Australia, seen then as the mother country and the colonial upstarts.

Hon Ivo Bligh's team which toured Australia 1882/83.

When Ivo goes back with the urn, the urn;
Studd, Steel, Read and Tylecote return;
The welkin will ring loud,
The great crowd will feel proud,
Seeing Barlow and Bates with the urn, the urn;
And the rest coming home with the urn.

As with 'The Ashes', so with Test matches which history has perhaps endowed with a significance they did not possess at the time. Certainly Charles Alcock was prescient enough to see a future in international sport, but, as home teams to play in these matches were at the time in England, Australia and South Africa picked by the executive of the ground hosting the match and the visiting side privately selected, it is difficult to avoid the conclusion that whatever the teams were called in the press they were not fully representative national sides.

So, on Saturday 30 December, on the MCG 'Australia' began the first Test match against 'England' with half a dozen players, including Read, making their international début in the first contest for the Ashes. No one knew it was a Test match; no one knew it was for the Ashes. Read made a modest 19 and 29 in a match which Australia won by 9 wickets, a result reversed three weeks later when the sides met again. This time Read's 75 was the top score on either side, as England recorded the first innings victory in a Test match, albeit billed in *Wisden* as the Hon Ivo Bligh's XI v Mr Murdoch's XI.

It was not a chanceless innings; he was dropped twice and a run-out chance missed.

> W.W.Read was batting in splendid form...Read got Palmer well away to the off for four followed by a straight drive for two. Read then played one into the slips and Barnes called for a run which Read refused, and both batsmen were at the same end. Horan, who had secured the ball, threw it badly to the bowler's wicket, and Spofforth being unable to reach it, Barnes got safely back to his own wicket.

The following day,

> runs came fast, principally through the agency of Read. When the Surrey amateur's score had reached 63, he drove one hard back to Giffen, but the bowler failed to hold it, and the batsman in return hit Palmer grandly to leg for 4.

Read played one back to Palmer, and had to retire for a well played innings of 75 (9 for 293).

The match also saw Test cricket's first hat-trick - by Willie Bates, who dismissed McDonnell, Giffen and Bonnor with consecutive balls - and Read was involved.

Bonnor played the first ball from Bates quietly into Read's hands at mid-on, close in, to the great satisfaction of the field, Bates having taken three wickets with successive balls.[110]

The third match of the series was played in Sydney - and again won by England, this time by 69 runs, Read making a significant contribution with joint top score (66 - with Tylecote in the first innings).

So, England won the rubber 2-1 and recaptured the Ashes, at some point on the tour a bail being burned to convert the concept into reality.

The three matches had been against W.L.Murdoch's team that had toured England - and indeed billed as 'English XI v Murdoch's Australian XI[111]: the Australian team had remained unchanged throughout the three matches of the series while England had made one change, Morley replacing Vernon for the second and third matches.

Fred Morley, the Nottinghamshire fast left-armer, had not in fact been fit enough to play in the first match, having broken a rib and being severely bruised in the collision between the *Peshawar* and the *Glen Roy*. They were injuries from which he never fully recovered and ones which contributed in part to his premature death two years later at the young age of thirty-three.

Unlike Morley, however, English cricket was not yet dead and on behalf of those who five months earlier had lamented it, *Cricket* waxed if not exactly lyrical, then at least loosely poetical.

NOT DEAD YET

HOORAY! English cricket is still "all alive oh!"
We thank you for proving that same Captain Ivo!
Played out? Many prigs, I confess to that tune, I confess, lie
But, faith, you'd convict 'em of 'bangs', dashing Leslie,
Or, if you should want further proof, why, I'll trouble you
A closer to read than Read W W. [112]

110   *Cricket* 16 March 1883
111   *Cricket* 16 March 1883
112   *Cricket* 16 March 1883

After cementing the series win, the team then travelled north to meet Eighteen of Queensland in Brisbane where Read again top-scored with 84 from a total of 265. It was, however, his innings of 66 in the next match against Eighteen of Maryborough which resulted in his owning a corner of a foreign field that was forever Australia.

> MR W W READ is now a landowner. His success in making the highest score at Maryborough in Queensland entitled him to an allotment of land valued at £25 in the township of Carolin, Queensland, offered by a syndicate to the most successful run-getter.[113]

Bligh's XI won by an innings and 58 runs, despite making only 179; the local side was clearly out of its depth, losing its 34 wickets for 121. Ironically, had it not been for a fairly relaxed approach to the Laws and conventions of the game, Read would not have been 'the most successful run-getter'. Not out overnight, he was late arriving at the ground next morning – but, rather than being ruled 'retired out', was allowed to continue his innings at the fall of the next wicket.

The award is an interesting forerunner of the cash, cars and mobile phones now dished out liberally by sponsors. The family has no record or recollection of the land being disposed of and it is theoretically possible that they own a bit of Australia, but it is a claim that they are unlikely to pursue as adverse possession and squatters' rights have had almost 130 years to kick in.

Then, with the informality that characterised nineteenth-century fixture planning, a fourth Test match was arranged against a 'combined' side which showed three changes, while England again remained unchanged. Australia won by four wickets, but to go with *Wisden*'s footnote that the match was not reckoned as one which counted towards an Ashes series[114] could be added a marginal note that as an experiment, each of the four innings was played on a separate pitch.

The novel idea of using four pitches was born not of an idle whim, but of controversy which arose in the third match when Barlow accused Spofforth of cutting up the pitch with his spikes and the Australian returned the compliment. Somehow, Read was on the periphery of the argument but declined to get involved.[115]

113   *Cricket* 19 April 1883
114   *Wisden* 2011 p 1376
115   Cashman, *The "Demon Spofforth"* p 138

According to the press

> After the match was over an allusion was made in conversation to Spofforth having cut up the wicket with his feet. This so annoyed the demon bowler that he struck out at Mr. Read, of the English eleven. Fortunately for Spofforth, the genial Surrey secretary is as good tempered as he is muscular and contented himself by smiling upon his ill mannered adversary.[116]

Read's version of events is different. He states that Barlow was the first to be accused, as a result of which, the counter-allegation was levelled against Spofforth.

> Here is a curious protest that was made in one of our matches: I think it was at Melbourne. It was alleged that the plates in Barlow's boots did great damage to the turf, and the English captain's attention was drawn to "Barlow's boots."

> The Hon Ivo Bligh, with great courtesy, had the offending plates removed, a proceeding which gave great umbrage to the wearer, who declared he had played with the same plates in his boots in all the county matches in England and that a suspicion of unfair play had never been entertained against him during his cricketing career at home. A counter-charge was now brought against Spofforth by several of the Englishmen, who accused that bowler of unlawfully putting spikes into his boots to cut up the turf. Spofforth brought evidence to show that he only used one nail and one spike – less than any other cricketer uses – in the present match. It was decided to leave the matter in the hands of the umpires, and if they saw a player using unfair means to cut up the turf, those functionaries had it in their power to stop the malpractice.[117]

Three days later, the satirical *Bulletin* reduced the episode to the farce it almost certainly was.

> Song of the Spike - A Cricketing Carol

> Twas in the dressing room, and lo,
> When all were gathered round
> Spoff cut up rough on Barlow 'cause
> He cut up rough the ground.

> "Those cursed spikes!" The Demon cried,

116   *The Age* 30 January 1883
117   *Annals of Cricket* p 170-171

"Have spoilt our chance you see!"
"About my spike then" Barlow said
"Just don't you spike to me."

"You ploughed it up then" Spofforth yelled
"Come! How would you have liked it?
Our chance has gone all through that spike,-
It's just what I ex-spike-ted."

"You lie!" cried Barlow, then Spoff shaped
Quite quick for the affray;
All thought that spike would cause a great
Spiketacular display.

Then Read appeared, and said "Oh bosh!
Of this spike we're all full;
To fight about a spike is not
A bit respiketable."'

"I'll go for you!" then howls out Spoff.
But Read said – "No, not quite,
I came out here for cricket, I
Did not come out to fight."[118]

For Read, the tour had been a successful one. As well as runs against the state sides and matches against the odds, he had made 228 in the Tests at an average of 32.57, second only to A.G.Steel. 'England' too had recovered some self-respect after events at the Oval in 1882 and, unlike some later tours, especially the one fifty years down the road, relations between the opposing camps seem, notwithstanding the 'spike' issue, to have remained entirely harmonious. At the farewell dinner, F.G.Smith (Sir William Clarke being unavoidably absent) addressed those assembled.

> He asked those present to join him in congratulating Mr Bligh on achieving his highest ambition in Australia, namely, the recovery of what had humorously been termed "the revered Ashes of English cricket" (Applause). It was his sincere conviction, and he was not afraid to express it, that their visitors having wrested those sacred relics from their previous possessors, they could only be regained in the old country, and if Australia wanted them, she would have to go to the old country for them.[119]

---

118   *Bulletin* 3 February 1883
119   *Cricket* 26 April 1883

This is one of few jocular earlier references to what was later to become a far more serious sporting icon.

During the 1883 season, in fact on the second day of Edward Pooley's benefit match, Read was presented with an illuminated inscription on vellum and 250 guineas (almost twice his annual salary as Assistant Secretary and about three times as much as many people earned in a year) to commemorate his batting in Australia. The scroll has survived and is in the hands of the family. To Pooley's benefit fund, the club added £25 to the £400 taken at the gate.

Despite Read's performances in Australia in 1882/83 and in the Anglo-Australian Tests in 1884, there was never any chance of his being selected for the 1884/85 tour – or indeed the later 1886/87 one. These were very much commercially orientated 'professional' tours, organised by Shaw, Shrewsbury and Lillywhite with the principal purpose of making money, and the professional-amateur balance was a mirror image of that which had obtained on Ivo Bligh's Ashes winning tour.

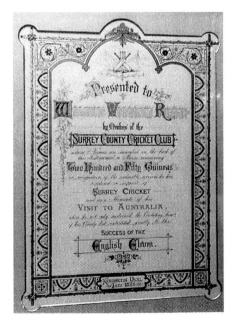

The vellum scroll presented by Surrey County Cricket Club to Read
in recognition of his performances in Australia in 1882/83.
[The Read Family]

1887/88

Australian politics spilled over into English cricket as what had been a possibility for the previous Australian season, but ultimately prevented by common sense, now became a reality and two English sides left literally simultaneously - indeed on the same ship – the *Iberia* - for the Antipodes. It was before the days of the Australian Cricket Board and the slightly earlier political federation of the states when tours were still privately organised, so two (or more!) parallel tours were within the realms of possibility. Shaw, Shrewsbury and Lillywhite were always on course to repeat their 1886/87 adventure, but as early as February 1887, *Cricket* was alive to the possibility of the farce of twin tours.

> On the other hand, the Committee of the Melbourne Club are equally determined to carry out their plan of bringing out a mixed team. Mr G F Vernon is acting on their behalf here and he will, in conjunction with W W Read, select the players. These will in all probability consist of nine amateurs and four professionals.

> It is of course very much to be regretted for obvious reasons that the possibility of two English teams simultaneously touring in Australia which everyone fondly hoped had been removed by the withdrawal of the Melbourne Club last season should have again arisen. It is not, we trust, too late even now, to arrive at some basis of agreement which will prevent such an alternative. The Melbourne Club as far as we can gather has, indeed, signified its readiness to act in conjunction with the Sydney Association to secure the presence of the strongest possible English combination in honour of the centennial year.[120]

The *Iberia* left Plymouth on 7 September and arrived in Adelaide some six weeks later, having stopped off at various points *en route*. There seems to have been a high degree of camaraderie between the two teams and some years later, Lord Hawke recalls the deck sports, the amateur dramatics and sharing a cabin with Read and Monty Bowden.

> Going through the Red Sea in September, three of us in a three-berth cabin did not provide much elbow-room, my companions being Walter Read and Monty Bowden. This was my initiation into deck sports and there was a big bout of

---

120   *Cricket* 24 February 1887

buffoonery when crossing the Line. It was jolly having twenty-six first class cricketers on a long trip, and many a cricket yarn was told and many a match discussed. Remembering what a distinguished actor C Aubrey Smith has become, it is interesting in my scrap-book to find a play-bill of amateur theatricals on board. Byron's farcical comedy "Old Soldiers" was performed and he it was who played the leading part, WW Read and Monty Bowden also being included in the cast.[121]

The party stopped briefly in Western Australia, spending time in the developing town of Albany where long walks and billiards filled in the afternoon. It was a less than fully fit team which eventually arrived at its destination, Read having sprained his ankle and Vernon having cut his ear as a result of falling down some steps. There was the usual welcome from civic dignitaries and representatives of the South Australian and Victorian Cricket Associations and the Melbourne Cricket Club. In the absence of the captain, the Hon M.B.Hawke, addressing a large public audience for the first time in his life (but certainly not the last), was upbeat and optimistic.

Speaking about the rival teams, he said that they had been on the most amicable terms on the voyage, in fact, had agreed that if arrangements could be made they would combine to meet the full strength of Australia in a series of test matches. Great applause greeted this remark. The suggestion had already been made in Melbourne and the MCC had stated they would have no objection. Mr Walter Read also responded in a few well-chosen words.[122]

They then adjourned to the Adelaide Oval for practice. WW took no part because of his injury, nor did he play in the opening match of the tour against South Australia, his first appearance being in the next against Victoria where he made a modest dozen in an innings victory.

His reputation had preceded him, however; 'Felix' (Thomas Horan), writing in the *Australasian* anticipated more significant contributions.

The great disappointment was W W Read who was then bowled by Boyle for 12. But then it should be remembered that this was his first appearance since he left the old country. When

---

121   *Recollections and Reminiscences* p 100 et seq
122   *Cricket* 29 December 1887

he runs into form, the bowlers will get it pretty hot from the Surrey crack.[123]

'Felix' was not wrong, as demonstrated by Read's average of 55.45 in first-class matches, including 183 against South Australia at the Adelaide Oval – an innings straddling Christmas Eve and Boxing Day with Christmas Day (a Sunday) off in between - in a five-day match eventually drawn after South Australia had followed on. Read's innings was eclipsed by George Giffen's second innings of 203. South Australia's 493 occupied 411.1 (four-ball) overs and spanned four days and ten and a half hours – riveting Christmas viewing. However, the over rate was 39 an hour, equivalent to 26 six-ball overs (and with more changeovers) – or about twice the rate in some present day first-class cricket. *Tempora mutantur.*

Martin Hawke had been obliged to return home after this match because of the sudden death of his father, leaving Vernon to captain the side in most of the tourists' matches, but providing the opportunity for Read to captain the combined 'England' side in the optimistically anticipated series of test matches, reduced eventually, alas, to a 'series' of one.

Although the two English teams amalgamated to produce a strong eleven for the Test match, the fragmented state of Australian cricket meant that a number of leading players did not make themselves available for the match which began at Sydney on 10 February and was billed as the Combined English team v New South Wales and Victoria. The visitors made a modest 113, the home side an even more modest 42 (still their lowest Test total at home); the second innings followed a similar pattern, as Turner and Ferris brought their match tally to eighteen wickets, to be matched by Lohmann and Peel as England won by 126 runs in what Cricket described as 'the most hollow fashion'.[124] So few were the batting achievements, that even a partnership of 18 between Shrewsbury and Read merited favourable comment in the media.

> Mr Walter Read, the captain, appeared. The best amateur and professional batsmen of England were now together, and the play of each was worthy of their great reputation.[125]

There was, however, plenty of cricket outside the Test match - seven first-class matches against the state sides and an Australian XI, plus a number of others against the odds. The

---

123   *Cricket* 29 December 1887
124   *Cricket* 29 March 1888
125   *Cricket* 29 March 1888

latter were sometimes taken less than seriously. Against XXII of Cootamundra, Read batted at No.11 and almost succeeded in seeing Bobby Abel, who carried his bat, to a century.

> Mr Walter Read, who went in last, did his best to enable his county comrade to attain his desire, but he was stopped after playing a good innings for 33.[126]

Record-keeping at the time being less meticulous than it has subsequently become, his dismissal is recorded in *Cricket Archive* as 'c [unknown]'.

After the Test match, a couple of Read centuries followed, firstly a second innings of 142 not out against Victoria,

> Mr Read opened, as is customary with him, cautiously. He was bent on a score as Shrewsbury, some 500 miles away was known to have made a tolerable number against New South Wales and the two are running for a place. When Mr Read sets to work with his whole heart, as George Giffen says, he is about the most difficult man in the world to bowl. At any rate, Victorians found him a hard nut... Mr Read and Peel then treated the bowling very cavalierly. The former especially was in great form to the delight of the few spectators. His innings which included fourteen boundary hits was the best he has ever played in Melbourne.[127]

Then 119 against New South Wales,

> Mr W Read came next and he very soon saw Abel give place to Mr O'Brien. Their partnership proved very advantageous, as the pair knocked the bowling all over the place, and nearly 100 runs were put on before Mr O'Brien was caught at the wicket. Mr Read continued to hit freely, and the score increased to 248, principally through his agency, before the next wicket fell. Rawlin succeeded Mr Newton, and only a few runs had been added when Mr Read was thrown out. He had played a splendid innings for 119, though he gave a fairly easy chance to Turner when he had scored a single.[128]

He had now scored a century against each of the three state sides and captained 'England' to a Test match victory. However 'hollow' the latter, it all added up to a successful trip after an unpromising start.

---

126   *Cricket* 29 March 1888
127   *Cricket* 26 April 1888
128   *Cricket* 29 March 1888

Owing to a severe attack of neuralgia, Mr W W Read was not in form and his ill success at the outset was the source of considerable disappointment to his many friends at home. As time advanced though, he settled down into quite his best style..... Three of the scores of a hundred made by the team were from his bat, and it is curious that he should have scored one in each of the three capitals of the Australian colonies, to wit, at Adelaide, Sydney and Melbourne. It is eminently satisfactory to report that this great English batsman fully upheld his high reputation during the winter. His fine average.... in representative matches is to be hoped an augury of an equally brilliant record for Surrey during the approaching English season.[129]

A decade later *Cricket* pointed out that Read was among a very small group of five amateurs who had made two trips to Australia. The others were W.G.Grace, G.F.Vernon, H.Philipson and A.C. MacLaren. Professionals on the other hand had made many more. Johnny Briggs was about to pay his sixth visit.

---

129   *Cricket* 26 April 1888

Chapter Seven
Surrey and England 1888/97

1888

Although his average was a little lower than the 40+ of the three preceding English seasons, Read recorded an individual score that was Surrey's highest at the time and only half-a-dozen shy of W.G.Grace's record of 344.

> Mr Read continued to score at a great rate, treating all the Oxford bowling with impartiality. Just as Mr Read was within six runs of reaching the highest score on record (Mr W G Grace's 344 for MCC and Ground v Kent at Canterbury in 1876) he got under one and was easily had at slip. His 338, the second highest innings recorded in a first-class match was a remarkable display of well-timed vigorous batting. He was six hours and a half at the wicket and except for two very hot returns, at 55 and 76, to Mr Forster, gave no chance. His score was made up of one 5, forty-six 4's, fourteen 3's, twenty-nine 2's and forty-nine singles. Surrey's total of 650 is the highest in an important match, though it has been twice beaten in Australia.[130]

Despite the advent of four-day cricket, better pitches and higher scores, Read's 344 remains the second highest individual innings in Surrey history, surpassed in 1899 by Abel's 357 against Somerset and, other than that, exceeded at The Oval only by Hutton's 364 in 1938 and Fairbrother's 366 in 1990.

In complete contrast, Read produced virtually the only batting performance of any note in the match at Old Trafford on 2 August when Lancashire were beaten in one day by an innings and 25 runs. It was George Lohmann's match in every way. He had eight for 13 followed by five for 38, but on what must have been the stickiest of sticky wickets, Read rose above the conditions to guide Surrey to a first innings lead of 88. It was enough.

---

130   *Cricket* 28 June 1888

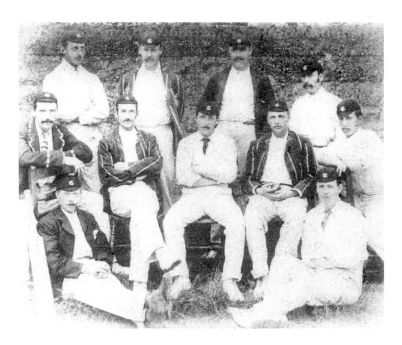

Surrey - Champion County (again) 1888.
[Surrey County Cricket Club]

No one stayed long with Mr Read, who carried out his bat for 49. Going in second wicket down, he was in while 101 runs were added, and considering the state of the ground, it was a display of very high merit. He did not seem to be troubled by the bowling at all, and his batting was marked by great judgment as well as freedom.[131]

In relaxed, end-of-season mood, he made a major contribution to the South's 47 run win over the North at the Hastings Festival.

Mr Read gave the Northern bowlers a lot of trouble, and his batting was decidedly the feature of the innings. He scored all round freely and the total had been raised to 233 before he was caught at slip, the ball going off his hand. He was only two hours and ten minutes at the crease for his 96 and as a display of free and powerful cricket, it was worthy of the highest praise. Among his hits was an on-drive from Peel out of the ground for six.[132]

---

131   *Cricket* 9 August 1888
132   *Cricket* 20 September 1888

✱Surrey County Cricket Club✱

1888.

Surrey v. Oxford University

KENNINGTON OVAL.

JUNE 25, 26 AND 27.

Drawn.

SURREY.

Abel, b Forster	...	97
Mr. J. Shuter, c Philipson, b Brown	...	24
Mr. K. J. Key, c Thesiger, b Forster	...	35
Mr. W. W. Read, c Forster, b Gresson	...	338
M. Read, c Forster, b Gresson	...	11
Lohmann, c Scott, b Brown	...	7
Henderson, c Croome, b Watson	...	36
Wood, c Simpson, b Brown	...	25
Mr. M. P. Bowden, c Cochrane, b Forster	...	21
Beaumont, not out	...	10
Bowley, c Gresson, b Forster	...	4
B 5, lb 7	...	12
		—
Total	...	650

1st Inns.—1 for 47, 2- 96, 3-233, 4-317, 5-339, 6-543, 7-606, 8-620, 9-646.

OXFORD UNIVERSITY.

E. T. B. Simpson, not out	...	15
F. H. Gresson, not out	...	30
B ...	...	2
		—
Total	...	47

Lord George Scott, W. Rashleigh, Hon. F. J. N. Thesiger, A. C. Croome, H. W. Forster, C. Wreford-Brown, A. K. Watson, H. Philipson and A. H. Cochrane did not bat.

WRIGHT & CO, 41, ST. ANDREW'S HILL, E.C.

Silk scorecard of Read's 338 v Oxford University at The Oval 1888.
[Surrey County Cricket Club]

1889

His performances the following season were less impressive. For the first time for seven seasons he failed to reach a thousand runs and made just one first-class century, 110 not out, in an innings victory over Middlesex at The Oval. Unlike the previous two years, Surrey failed to emerge as Champion County and after some debate, there was a tripartite split between Surrey, Lancashire and Nottinghamshire, leading to the abandonment of the informal method where the award was made by the press – not always unanimously (see footnote to 1887 season) – and the inauguration of the County Championship the following season.

He did, however, achieve something unique for Surrey at the time, albeit not in a first-class match, a century in each innings – 105 and 130 - against the touring Gentlemen of Philadelphia.

In the autumn he again attended the meeting of County Secretaries,[133] but not the newly-established Cricket Council. That was left to the captain and the secretary.

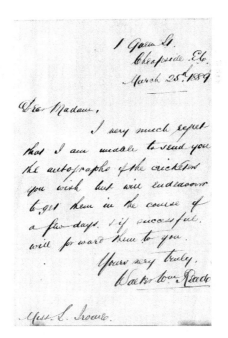

Example of Read's handwriting - and helpfulness - March 1889.
[Surrey County Cricket Club]

---

133   *Cricket* 27 September 1889

1890

Before the county season got under way, Read played for Lord Sheffield's XI against the Australians in their opening match at Sheffield Park. He was part of a team that lost by an innings and 34 runs after being bowled out for 27 in the first innings. Read made no contribution to that total; Grace made 20. More serious cricket lay ahead in the first year of the newly-established points-based County Championship which Surrey were to win for its first three years.

Although WW was never again to scale the heights of batting achieved in the middle of the decade, he still remained highly competent and, in another low-scoring encounter on another Old Trafford 'sticky', demonstrated once again that his talents were not limited to fast scoring against modest attacks on good pitches. Unlike the equivalent fixture in 1888, the match did extend to a second day, but 'nobbut just' as they say in the vernacular around those parts. Twenty-nine wickets fell on the first day, there were fewer than three hundred runs in the four completed innings and three overs by Barlow apart, Briggs and Watson for Lancashire, Lohmann and Sharpe for Surrey bowled throughout the match. In the first innings as Surrey were bowled out for 69, WW stood alone amid the carnage.

> Briggs and Watson were very difficult and except Mr W W Read who made 30 out of 35 when he was in, there was not a double figure in the innings, which only lasted an hour and fifty minutes.[134]

Lancashire were dismissed on the second morning, all ten being bowled. Lohmann had 7 for 21, to give him match figures of 13 for 54.

Read played in both Test matches that summer, but made negligible contributions to England's wins, by seven wickets at Lord's and two at The Oval. Neither he nor George Lohmann was able to repeat their heroics at Old Trafford, the match there being abandoned without a ball bowled.

The end of the season is inevitably a time for reminiscences and *Cricket* has the following one from the Hastings Festival when, recalling festivals of earlier years,

> I saw W W Read knock the ball out of the Hastings ground bang

---

134   *Cricket* 12 June 1890

up the water spout – for carrying off the rain – attached to a house outside and opposite the ground; the said ball being afterwards fielded out of the spout with the help of a ladder, by a man who threw it back again into the ground, amid tumultuous applause.[135]

Six years later, in his *Annals of Cricket*, Read relates the same incident in almost exactly the same terms, with only minor changes to vocabulary and punctuation.[136]

This year too he played his part in entertaining the crowds. The South beat the North by the narrow margin of nine runs, the contribution of the Surrey contingent, Read in particular being significant.

> Though the South had a very useful majority of 58 runs to help them in their second innings, the majority of the batsmen found the light late on Friday afternoon very troublesome and but for the Surrey men who had done the bulk of the run-getting on the previous day they would have fared very badly. As it was Mr Read, Lohmann and Abel between them were responsible for 91 out of 115 from the bat, and Mr Read's share was nearly one half of the entire total. His play was worthy of unstinted praise..... as will be seen he scored altogether in the match 146 for once out. On Friday, too, his play was absolutely without fault, and his brilliant performance will be a source of satisfaction to all classes of cricketers.[137]

A not dissimilar eulogy was included in the *Sporting Life*, the 'Man on the Spot' producing the following lines:

TO MR WALTER READ

See him make his boundary cuts,
He ain't the sort to play for nuts:
Hooks 'em here and carves 'em there,
Bungs 'em off and hits 'em square:
And when I shed my little bob,
I like to see him "on the job".[138]

The rhyming couplets would not be a candidate for the Pulitzer Prize for Poetry, but the sentiment is clear enough.

---

135   *Cricket* 11 September 1890
136   p 184
137   *Cricket* 18 September 1890
138   *Sporting Life* p 182

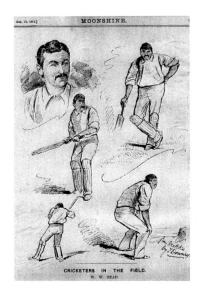

A Cartoonist's view of Read in Moonshine *22 August 1891.*

1891

With Lohmann and Sharpe to the fore, Surrey dominated and won the County Championship, though for Read it was another modest season - 831 first-class runs at an average of 23.08 with a highest score of 77 after a first-innings duck for the Gentlemen in an innings defeat by the Players at Hastings.

Earlier the Gentlemen dominated the equivalent fixture against the Players at The Oval, winning by an innings and 54 runs, Read 'taking out his bat for an extremely well played fifty' in a total of 258.[139]

Unusually, in the Gentlemen of England (albeit with two Australians and an Irishman) v Mordecai Sherwin's Nottinghamshire XI match at Scarborough, Read distinguished himself with the ball. In a career spanning a quarter of a century, his batting was of world-class standard, his fielding well above the norm, but his slow lobs brought him only 108 first-class wickets including 6-24, a career best, three of them in as many balls in this match.

---

139   *Cricket*   9 July 1891

The scorecard read:

W Barnes	c Stoddart b Read	17
W Attewell	b Read	0
F Dixon	b Read	0

3-51, 4-51, 5-51[140]

In his Introduction to *Annals of Cricket*, John Shuter gives the hat-trick victims as Dixon, Barnes and Gunn.[141] Read did take Gunn's wicket, but the following day for 40, after he had been 26 not out overnight in a total of 60-6. So, given the fall of the three wickets at 51, Gunn could not have been part of the hat-trick. In the second innings Read made 52, increasing his contribution to a convincing 115 run win by his team.

1892

After three relatively lean years the South African tour of the previous winter seems to have led to an improvement in form and 1892 saw something of a revival in Read's batting fortunes.

After a fairly ordinary start to the season, he moved up the order, from his regular position at No.4 to opening the innings with Bobby Abel. The experiment was an instant success, as indeed it had been five years earlier when, after a similar run of poor form, he had opened against Kent and made a century.

His 196 not out against Sussex was, after two seasons without a century, one of three and his highest since his near-record 338 against Oxford University in 1888. It followed upon 112 against the same opponents a week earlier and each contributed to innings victories over Surrey's south coast neighbours.

> Though the wicket at first was a trifle slow, Mr Read and Abel, who began the batting for Surrey, did not find it difficult. On the contrary, they both scored freely and the score which at luncheon time was 118, was raised to 156 before Abel was out. The two batsmen had been together two hours and ten minutes and Abel's share of the total was 61.... Altogether he had been batting just under three hours and his 112 was altogether worthy of his best days.[142]

Then, a week later, he 'continued to bat in admirable style and

---

140   *Cricket Archive*
141   So does Read – almost certainly Shuter's source – in an interview in *Cricket* 23 May 1895
142   *Cricket* 21 July 1892

though unlucky enough to miss his second hundred by four, carried out his bat.'[143] A match-winning 75 and 32 against Yorkshire followed, as inevitably did the poetry.

I wish to direct CRICKET- readers' attention

To a three-figure score
We can hardly ignore –
To the rhyme-slinger's mind it's well worthy of mention.

. . . .

As witness this week on the Kennington ground,
Where proof of his prowess the Sussex men found,
When "W.W." kept up his sticks
Till he'd notched up a nice hundred and ninety-six,

And might have made more,
For he *has* such a way with him,
But the innings was o'er –
There were none left to stay with him
Which seems to suggest that the Reigate crack
To his old time form is coming back.

The doggerel goes on to suggest, however, that although 196 not out is a nice little average improver, it may not count, as MCC may well decide retrospectively that Sussex is a second-class county, a cynical reference to the ongoing debate within and around MCC as to whether the two Surrey-Scotland matches that year should be granted first-class status. Eventually, they were not, doubtless a correct decision in the light of Surrey's win by an innings and 247 runs, but detrimental to WW's average, as he had an impressive 156 in Edinburgh against an unchallenging Scottish attack.

Baldwin and Mr Read put on 69 for the first wicket and as the majority of the eleven scored well against the modest bowling of Scotland, the total reached the high figure of 391. The great feature of the innings was the brilliant display of Mr Read, an innings of three hours and a quarter, with only one real mistake and that in the long field when he had made 109. In the early part of his innings he played with care but when he had got set he hit all round in his very best style and in the last hour and a half scored 95 of his runs.

143   *Cricket* 28 July 1892

The Surrey team in 1892.
[Surrey County Cricket Club]

Read, himself, was clearly satisfied with both his own and the team's form.

> The Surrey eleven had a magnificent season in 1892, and richly deserved to retain the championship. Fine all-round cricket on the part of the whole team was the main cause of Surrey's consistent success but two members of the eleven – Lockwood and Lohmann – had certainly a far larger share than any of their colleagues in winning the matches. I came back to something very like my best form. After one or two moderately good scores I played an innings of 75, not out, *(sic)* to win the match against Middlesex at the Oval, on the 14th of June, and from that time until the end of the season I was in good heart, scoring no fewer than four innings of over a hundred, including 196 not out against Sussex at the Oval, and 156 against Scotland at Edinburgh.[144]

His 107 against Gloucestershire too was indicative of his dominance of Surrey's batting that year.

> Mr Read was in his very best form and all the bowling came alike to him. Lohmann too was in a hitting vein, and while he was in with Mr Read 68 runs were put on in thirty minutes. Mr Read has rarely been seen to better advantage. He was only in

---

144   *Annals of Cricket* pp184-185. In fact he was dismissed

for an hour and fifty minutes and in this time scored as many as 107 out of 169 runs. All round his hitting was very hard and well timed, and to our knowledge, he gave no chance.[145]

In making Read one of its five batsmen of the year, *Wisden* too was appropriately effusive.

Mr. W W Read, to the great delight of all supporters of Surrey cricket came back to his best form. He began the season under discouraging conditions, for during his winter trip at the Cape he had done nothing to sustain his reputation, and fears were entertained that his long and brilliant career was drawing to a close. Any such idea, however, had been completely dissipated before the summer was far advanced. After one or two moderately good scores which indicated that he was himself again, he played a splendid innings of 75 not out *(sic)* to win the match against Middlesex at the Oval on the 14th of June, and from that time until the end of the season he did great things, scoring no fewer than four innings of over a hundred -112 against Sussex at Brighton; 196 not out against Sussex at the Oval; 156 against Scotland at Edinburgh; and 107 against Gloucestershire at Cheltenham. As the result of these and other good performances he came out at the top of the batting, both in first-class county fixtures and all matches, averaging in the one over 40 runs an innings and in all matches over 35. Such a record in the case of a batsman whose first appearance in a big match dates as far back as 1873 was as remarkable as it was gratifying. The confidence born of success enabled him to play the vigorous forcing game that is natural to him. There was nothing of the over-caution which, to our thinking, seriously prejudiced his efforts in 1891. Surrey has never had so fine a batsman, and everyone was delighted to see him, after a brief period of depression again assert himself as one of the great cricketers of the day. Between him and the other batsmen on the side there was a very considerable gap...[146]

His three centuries were as many as his colleagues scored between them that season, and while statistics may not tell everything, the gap between Read's average of 40 and, in second place, Abel's of 25 tells a lot.

The season was not entirely one of unbroken success, however. Against Notts Read and Abel got themselves into a tangle over a

---

145   *Cricket* 25 August 1892
146   *Wisden* 1893 p 4. In fact Read was dismissed.

second run. The wicket was put down with both men out of their creases. Both began to walk off until the umpire was appealed to and he decided that it was Read who was run out.[147]

Read's batting and Lohmann's bowling were once again contributory factors to yet another County Championship, Surrey's fifth in six seasons with a shared one in between.

1893

1893 saw only one century, but a batting average still over 30 and his highest first-class run aggregate for five seasons.

His sole century that season was made at Old Trafford in a seven wicket victory over the red rose county.

> ...Mr Read was able to carry out his bat. A better display of cricket than his 174[148] there could not be. From the first he was quite at home with the Lancashire bowling as he scored freely all round the wicket. Though he was batting for three and a half hours in all he hardly made a faulty stroke, none that could be called a chance.[149]

Cricket being the great leveller that it is, he came down to earth in the second innings, bowled by Mold for a duck. It did not matter. By that stage victory was in sight.

However, the following week on the other side of the Pennines at Bramall Lane, it was a different story. Surrey lost by 58 runs in an encounter in which the four completed innings totalled but 320, Richardson and Lockwood cleaning up for Surrey, Hirst and Wardall doing likewise for the home side, Read was the only Surrey batsman to twice reach double figures.

Likewise, later in the season, Read demonstrated, by no means for the first time in his career, that his batting was not all about rapid scoring. He had the ability and the temperament to occupy the crease when required. Against Somerset at The Oval

> Key and W W Read were the first to make a stand but it was not until Brockwell came in at the fall of the fifth wicket that Surrey seemed to have an outside chance. WW was in two hours and a quarter for his 28.[150]

147   David Kynaston *Bobby Abel, Professional Batsman* p 38
148   *sic* – actually 147 not out
149   *Cricket* 15 June 1893
150   *Cricket* 20 July 1893

It was all to no avail. Surrey lost by 29 runs.

With Lohmann absent in South Africa afflicted by the early stages of tuberculosis and seeking an improvement in his health, it was a poor season for Surrey. They slipped to fifth place in the Championship.

In representative cricket, however, Read played a large part in the Gentlemen v Players at Lord's.

> Though eight of the eleven got double figures the bulk of the scoring was done by the two Surrey cricketers, W W Read and Wells. The former has rarely been seen to better advantage, and his 79 was an innings in every way up to his best standard.[151]

For England too, he still had something to offer. It was long before central contracts were thought of, and teams dubbed 'England', 'Australia' and 'South Africa' were often dependent on players being released by their counties, states or provinces. At the meeting of county secretaries in December 1892, there was an agreement that 'England' should take priority. It was no more than a gentlemen's agreement, however, and in no way legally enforceable, as convincingly demonstrated by Yorkshire when Wainwright was withheld from the Oval Test team of 1893. He was replaced by Flowers but when the latter was taken ill on the first morning of the match, WW was on hand to fill the vacancy and prolong an international career which he must have thought was already over. He was one of six England batsmen to score more than fifty - and it was enough to give him another match at Old Trafford before the final curtain fell on his Test match appearances.

The Oval Test was the Benefit Match for Maurice Read. Walter and he shared a surname and on occasions, partnerships, but although one ill-informed journalist had assumed they were brothers, they were not related. Maurice must have been pretty satisfied with the outcome. The Australians took half the gate, but attendances of 12,720 on the first day, 13,061 on the second and 2,471 on the third as England completed an innings victory plus a large subscription list bagged him an above average £ 1,200.

The Old Trafford match was drawn to give England a 1-0 series victory. They never looked like losing the match and may well have won it, had it not been for some end of second innings

---

151   *Cricket* 13 July 1893

defiance by Turner and Blackham. Read's Test career ended with a
0 not out in a match more memorable for Old Trafford's first Test
match century - by William Gunn - and Tom Richardson's two five
wicket hauls on his Test début.

1894

Now in his twenty-second season and thirty-ninth year, Read was
inevitably past his best, but he still came out with the highest
average for Surrey and there were still some memorable moments.
He scored 60 for the Gentlemen at the Oval and what was now
becoming his annual century was a big and match-winning one.
Against Yorkshire at the Oval

> Mr W W Read who has been out of luck in the previous matches,
> was this time in his best form and Brockwell and he punished
> the Yorkshire bowling severely....

> Mr Read completed his hundred after he had been in two
> hours.

> Mr Read was out unluckily. He played a ball from Hirst on to
> his foot and thence on to his wicket. The outgoing batsman has
> never in his long career been seen to better advantage. After
> the first few overs he played with consummate judgment as
> well as rare confidence and his hitting all round was up to his
> very best standard which is saying a great deal.[152]

His 161 was by some distance the highest score in the match,
Brockwell's the only other century, and contributed to a total of
401 which was almost sufficient to ensure an innings win. As it
was, Surrey won by ten wickets with a day to spare.

He had the top score of 33 not out in Surrey's second innings
against Lancashire when, after losing the first day's play to the
weather, Lancashire were bowled out for 74 in the fourth innings
to produce a tie. (There has been only one since then in Surrey
first-class matches). This was a match judged by Read later to be
the most exciting in which he had ever played.[153]

1895

For some years, it had been received opinion that the powers of
W.G.Grace were declining - unsurprisingly as he was now well into

---

152   *Cricket* 28 June 1894
153   *Cricket* 23 May 1895

The Surrey team in 1895.
[Surrey County Cricket Club]

his fifth decade. However, he defied the passing years and became the first player, at the age of forty-six to score a thousand runs in May. In 1866 he had played for England against Surrey. He remained the only surviving member of the twenty-two players that took part in that match when it was resurrected for Read's testimonial almost three decades later.

It may seem a contradiction to have a testimonial match for an amateur player, but there had never been any pretence that Read was an amateur in any except a technical sense. In his correspondence, Charles Alcock refers to 'Read's benefit', so there is no real difference between what was arranged for The Oval on 27 to 29 May and a benefit match for a professional, except that professionals did not have matches specially arranged for them. They simply took the gate, less expenses, from a county match, usually Yorkshire or Nottinghamshire. Maurice Read was allowed a Test match, a privilege later denied to George Lohmann, despite an initial promise of an Australian match.

The testimonial match was well organised, well publicised and successful.

The well deserved recognition of the invaluable services rendered by Mr W W Read to Surrey cricket for over twenty years, rendered the selection of this particular fixture for his testimonial match especially fitting.[154]

As a contest, the match was a non-event from the time that the Surrey openers, Abel and Lockwood were both dismissed without scoring. Although, thanks almost entirely to the bowling of Richardson, who had 6-105 in this match, Surrey were to reassume their accustomed position at the head of the Championship table, the days were long gone when they could expect to give 'England' a decent game. Surrey collapsed to the bowling of Arthur Pougher, who returned career best figures of 9-34, for 85; thanks in the main to Albert Ward's century, England replied with 363. The county did rather better in their second innings, but could muster only 203 to lose by an innings and 75 runs.

Read's contribution was three and one, plus eleven wicketless overs; but in financial terms, he had no cause for complaint. The gate was £843 18s 6d which, after the deduction of expenses of £140 11s, left him with £703 7s 6d to which could be added £125 15s subscribed by members.

He was later to have an influence on Surrey's young batsmen, but it comes as a surprise to learn that he inspired a future bowler. Anthony Meredith alludes to Read's interest in Digby Jephson and suggests that the elder man was something of a mentor to the younger and provided the initial encouragement to become a lobster. Read, of course, was an occasional lob bowler who was good enough to have taken a first-class hat-trick and had once dismissed Charles Kortright with a lob after he had hit Richardson, Lockwood and other Surrey bowlers all round the Oval.[155]

Cricket ran a feature looking at first-class averages over the twelve seasons, 1882-93. For Surrey, it was no surprise that Read came out top and when the net was cast wider and his performance compared with other leading players of his generation, he came behind Shrewsbury and Grace, but ahead of Gunn and Stoddart. On the amateur side, he was, as the Surrey CCC minutes record, 'second to but one'.

There were, however, moves to terminate Read's contract and negotiations on the terms of that went on over a couple of years.

154 *Cricket* 30 May 1895
155 Meredith *The Demon and the Lobster* p 50

He continued to play most 1st XI matches, and although his form was less consistent than it had been, once again he did not let the season pass without recording a century, this time against Sussex at Brighton when recalled because of a poor run of form by Leveson-Gower.

> Read gave no chance that went to hand, but during the last half-hour the bowling was punished with such severity that 46 runs were added and at last the Surrey score had been carried to 346 with Abel, not out 138 and Read, not out, 89. On Friday morning a lot of curiosity existed as to how Abel and Walter Read would increase the partnership, as overnight, they had put on 148 runs. The two men were not destined to stay much longer together, the score only having been carried to 357 when Abel was cleverly run out by Butt. The stand for the fourth wicket yielded 159, the runs having been obtained in rather more than two hours....just after Holland came in, Read completed his 100, ...Read's career was brought to a close by a catch at extra mid-of [sic] at 375. The innings of 111, which occupied him only two hours and a half, was in every way, worthy of Read's reputation. He gave no real chance, and played with all his old vigour and determination. Among his hits were fourteen 4's, four 3's and twelve 2's.[156]

1896

Notwithstanding negotiations on financial matters described elsewhere, Read managed to play more or less a full season and for the fourth season in succession recorded just a single century. It was made in adverse circumstances when he was not at his fittest.

> Mr W W Read was not well, and indeed he was doubtful whether to go in to bat. It was fortunate for Surrey that he did, for he soon settled down; his strokes all round were very hard, and he was quickly catching Abel when the latter was bowled. In proof of the lively character of the batting during the partnership, it may be stated that in an hour and thirty-five minutes the two batsmen had added 142 runs... Mr Read was ninth out at 348... He was only in two hours and twenty minutes for his 112, a substantial display of all round batting quite in his very best form.[157]

---

156   *Cricket* 5 September 1895
157   *Cricket* 7 May 1896.

1896 saw his last appearance in a Gentlemen v Players fixture. Appropriately it was at The Oval; appropriately too, he signed off with a fifty and was dismissed by Surrey colleagues Richardson in the first innings and Lohmann in the second – the future and the past of Surrey's attack. The Gentlemen scraped home by one wicket after the ninth wicket had fallen with the scores level.

It was, said *Cricket*, not the best season for captain Kingsmill Key. Neither was it for Surrey who after a sound start lost seven Championship matches and finished fourth in the table. Nor was it for Walter Read –

> The same remark applies to Mr Read, who though he was making runs all through the season, seldom showed his true form.[158]

His first-class batting average of 22.71 was the lowest since his appointment as Assistant Secretary enabled him to become a regular member of the Surrey team fifteen years earlier.

Lillywhite's, however, edited by Charles Alcock, remained politely complimentary.

> Plays very straight, and hits all round with great freedom; a fine field anywhere and can also keep wicket.[159]

The Surrey team in 1896.
[Surrey County Cricket Club]

---

158   *Cricket* 3 September 1896
159   1897 edition p 259

1897

...was his last season in first-class cricket. It started with a spot of illness and convalescence.

> W W READ who is getting over a rather bad bout of influenza, was off yesterday to Paris for a short holiday to recuperate, in view of the approaching strain of a heavy cricket season. Captain Key and H D G Leveson-Gower will be the other amateur regular members of the Surrey Eleven this summer. It is just on the cards that a fourth amateur, in the person of a well-known young cricketer may also find a place.[160]

The fourth amateur to whom reference is made is probably H.B.Chinnery who was to play 30 matches for the county over the next eight seasons.

> There was one little contrast at the Oval on Tuesday that tickled me a good deal, though it appeared to pass unnoticed by the crowd. After lunch, the first players to return to the field were the Surrey captain and WW, who strolled out together in earnest confab. They had scarcely reached the wicket when out of the pavilion side by side came Leveson-Gower and Chinnery. Old Surrey and young Surrey and what a contrast. By the two burly, stalwart veterans the youngsters looked slim undeveloped boys. Are they likely in days to come, I wonder, to approach the great deeds of their elder comrades? Leveson-Gower may be a worthy successor to Key; but one doubts if Chinnery will ever be a Walter Read. The Oval authorities have a high opinion of him, though, I know, and there is no mistake about his keenness.[161]

Read was about to retire with iconic status, the gold standard against which future aspirants were measured.

> I was talking of the veterans and especially Mr Walter Read, one of my earliest cricket heroes, and one in whose doings my interest has never varied. The great things which he has done for the county are almost innumerable, but they appear to be almost forgotten...There is a list of just fifty centuries, nearly four-fifths of them made in matches as to whose first-class calibre there can be no difference of opinion. No other player, save WG and Arthur Shrewsbury, can show such a

---

160   *Cricket* 15 April 1897
161   *Cricket* 13 May 1897

record, though I admit that the Indian Prince's beating it is only a matter of time.[162]

It was time to move on, time to pass on the torch to the younger generation. Appropriately, Read's farewell appearance was in the same fixture as the first – Yorkshire at The Oval. On the first occasion Yorkshire had won by nine wickets; this time it was a draw. Read began with three and ended with a single. Of the twenty-two players who took the field in 1873, only Read had survived the intervening twenty-four years. His 31 first-class centuries for Surrey were about a quarter of the total scored for the county.

H.S.Altham had no reservations about the rôle Read's batting had played in their Championship successes.

> In batting as in bowling, Surrey in their great years were blessed with one pre-eminent match-winner, Walter Read, easily the greatest run-getter in the county's history up till that date, and probably the finest batsman that had appeared in its ranks since William Beldham. In him defence and attack were admirably combined, and few amateurs have excelled him for consistency over a long period of years; but most of all will he be remembered for the power and frequency of his driving, at first straight and to the off, but towards the end of his career favouring the pull, of which he became the greatest known exponent, and eventually something of a slave.[163]

Read himself explains:

> ..that stroke was the outcome of experience. The idea lay dormant in my mind for some time, then I began to work it out. When I saw nearly all the fieldsmen on the 'off-side', I thought...'What a glorious chance for the man who can safely play the ball to the on'. One side was safeguarded everywhere, the other was the yawning gulf. So it occurred to me that it was possible to 'pull' balls from the 'off' to the 'on' side. I know it was not considered orthodox cricket, but it brought me runs and that was the main thing.[164]

He had had a huge impact, both on the field and off. In an obituary of Thomas Padwick, *Cricket* commented:

---

162   *Cricket* 27 May 1897
163   *Altham History of Cricket* pp173-174
164   *Cricket* 23 May 1895

Not many years ago he arranged a banquet in honour of Mr Walter Read, at Laker's Hotel, Redhill, which was presided over by the Mayor of Reigate.[165]

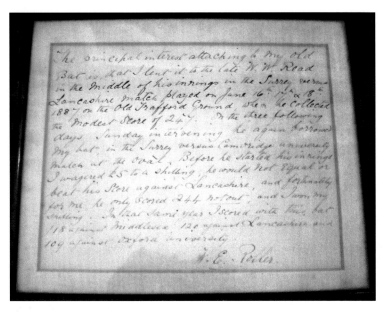

W.E.ROLLER describes how he lent his bat to WW and how he came close to losing a substantial bet.
[Surrey County Cricket Club]

---

165   *Cricket*   5 May 1898

Chapter Eight
South Africa 1891/92

Early in 1891, there was talk of Lohmann taking a team to South Africa. In the event it did not happen, as Lohmann went off to Australia with W.G.Grace, leaving the way clear for Read to captain a tour to the Cape organised by Edwin Ash, for some years a member of the Surrey committee, the founder of the Richmond Athletic Association and formerly Honorary Secretary of the infant Rugby Union. He had previously taken charge of a rugby tour to South Africa. In playing terms, the Ash-Read tour was a successful one, although finding the right footwear to cope with the novelty of matting wickets proved a challenge. Derbyshire professional, William Chatterton, in a 'chat' with W.A.Bettesworth says:

> None of us were well equipped for the game as it is played in South Africa. We had canvas boots which proved very awkward and were inclined to slip. At the same time, if you used nails you ran a great risk of ricking yourself. The best thing we found was a good heavy pair of lawn-tennis boots with india-rubber soles.[166]

The team left in November. Spirits seemed high and the tour was an adventure both on and off the field.

> On Saturday morning at twenty minutes to twelve o'clock a team under the Captaincy of Mr W.W.Read left Waterloo Station for Southampton to join the "Dunottar Castle" *en route* for South Africa. Mr Read, in addition to the two Australian cricketers, Messrs W.L.Murdoch and J.J. Ferris, is accompanied by Mr G. Brann of Sussex and the following professionals. F. Martin (Kent), J.T.Hearne (Middlesex), W.Chatterton (Derbyshire), A.D.Pougher (Leicestershire), G.G.Hearne (Kent), Alec Hearne (Kent), V. (late Bomber) Barton (Kent), H. Wood (Surrey), W. Brockwell (Surrey) and E. Leaney (Kent).[167]

---

166   *Chats on the Cricket Field* p 164
167   *Cricket 26 November 1891.* George Ayres (Surrey), not mentioned here, was also a member of the party.

The team which Read led to South Africa in 1891/92.

En route, Read celebrated his thirty-sixth birthday and updating his biography and quoting a contemporary newspaper, Haygarth said:

'Monday, November 23rd, is Mr W.W. Read's birthday, and many were the congratulations he received. Our gallant captain is in the height of good humour and spirits, and so are all our men in fact. Just before dinner we made a present to 'W.W.,' subscribed for by all our men, and with which Mr. Read seemed greatly pleased. It took the form of a silver match box and referee's whistle, and with it the following address: 'Presented to W.W.Read, Esq., by the members of the team of English cricketers, of which he is captain, visiting South Africa in the season of 1891-92, on the occasion of his birthday, during the voyage, on the 23rd November, 1891, as a small token of the esteem and regard in which he is held by them, and wishing him very many happy returns of the day.' Here followed the signature of each individual player.'[168]

There were the usual deck sports en route which doubtless doubled as bonding exercises and demonstrated that the amateurs were no less fit than the professionals. Of the eighteen competitive

---

168   *Scores and Biographies* Vol XIV p xcvi

events mentioned in *Cricket*, the cricketers either won or were well placed and other passengers appear not to have had a look-in.

During the voyage, three cricket matches were played against the officers of the ship, and in each case with the same natural result, the defeat of the sailors. Some sports were held on November 30 and December 4 with Mr W.W.Read as starter, Mr Murdoch and the chief officer of the ship as judges. The card comprised eighteen events and some of the best prizes were won by members of the eleven. Mr Brann won the half mile in fine style. The potato race to F. Martin with V. Barton second. J.T.Hearne, who was second in the half-mile walking race, won the high jump easily, Hearne second. W. Chatterton won the standing long jump, as well as the sprint race, twice round the deck, with J.T. Hearne and F. Martin in the order named. Putting the weight fell to the captain of the team, Mr W.W.Read, Mr G. Brann a good second. Mr J.J.Ferris took second prize for skipping, and Mr F.Martin was third in putting the bar. The tug-of-war was won by the first-class eight (including seven of the cricket team) who gained the second and third pulls. On December 4, W. Chatterton and A.D.Pougher won the Double Quoits. W.Brockwell was beaten in the final of the singles by only two points. The winners in the whist tournament turned up in G.Ayres and W. Brockwell.[169]

On arrival in Cape Town they were met by officials of the Western Province Club, including W.H.Milton. Also in the welcoming party were Frank Hearne, later to play against them and Surrey cricketer, Charles Mills, also earning a crust 'pro-ing' and coaching in South Africa.

The first matches, against Eleven of Cape Town, then Fifteen of Cape Colony, played just before and just after Christmas, were both drawn.

The Cricket Annual summarised the tour as follows:

The team taken out to South Africa by Mr. W W Read was all-round a stronger side than its predecessor in 1888-9 under the leadership of Major Warton, and its success in the field, notwithstanding the progress in cricket made by the colony during the interval, was certainly much more pronounced..... Altogether twenty matches were played, of which thirteen were won and the remaining seven drawn. Of the undecided games

---

169   *Cricket* 31 December 1891

Our mules require
a friendly lead

An awkward predicament

*Interesting predicaments as envisaged by The Cricket Field's cartoonist
in illustrations to George Brann's article on the tour.*

four would certainly have gone in favour of Mr. Read's side had there been time to finish them; another, that against 22 of Border District would probably also have been won; and in the remaining two, in which the Orange Free State and Griqualand West adopted the closure against their visitors, it is not by any means certain that the Colonists would have been successful in the end. Only one eleven a-side match was played, the last one of the tour, against a team representing the whole of South Africa, but the result, which afforded Mr. Read's team the biggest victory they had gained, must have been disappointing for the Colonists. It is but fair to them, however, to state that their side was not so strong as it could have been made, the most notable absentee being A B Tancred, who has the reputation of being the best all-round player in South Africa. The Englishmen were received everywhere with the utmost enthusiasm, and were entertained with unbounded hospitality, and it seems very evident that one of the results of the visit will be to largely encourage the development of the game in the South African colonies.[170]

In the sole Test, the second time Read had captained 'England', he maintained his 100% record. Against a very weak South African side, it would have been difficult to do otherwise. His team scored 369 against 97 and 83, Ferris bowling through the match to take 13 wickets for 91. He himself made 40, his Surrey colleague, wicket-keeper, Harry Wood 134 not out. In days when international qualification was more flexible, Ferris and Murdoch, who kept wicket in the second innings, had previously played for Australia, Frank Hearne making his début for South Africa had previously played for England. The Hearne family provided the two sides with three brothers and a cousin. Within a week, another team, subsequently called 'England' had beaten a team called 'Australia' by a rather larger margin. It all makes a bit of a nonsense of any trans-generation international statistical comparisons.

Of those playing in this match, fourteen were making their Test début. In retrospect, it borders on the farcical that this match and other nineteenth-century ones against South Africa have been given Test match status. The opinion among English cricketers who had played against the South Africans was that they were club standard, perhaps just below second-class county standard.[171] The South African team that toured the British Isles two years

---

170   p 302
171   *Cricket Quarterly* Vol 2 p 249

later in 1894, played no first-class matches, and that of 1901, while playing the counties in first-class fixtures, had no aspiration to anything like Test matches. *The Cricket Quarterly* argued strongly that South African matches before 1907 should be disregarded in Test match records. Bill Frindall, on the other hand, took the view that the status of those early matches had been sanctified by time.[172]

The tour had its trials and tribulations, though was not without its lighter side, as J.J.Ferris recalls in his chat with W.A.Bettesworth.

Did you enjoy your tour with Mr. WW Read's team in South Africa?

Very much indeed. The coach-riding was the only unpleasant part of the tour. Over one journey, which was supposed to take thirty-six hours, we took five days, which was no joke, as there were no conveniences for washing on the way. In the middle of the night we were obliged to get up sometimes to whip the mules, or else they would not have moved at all. One night we put up at a farmhouse, and Murdoch and I had a room to ourselves. There was only one bed, which looked anything but safe, so I proposed that Murdoch, being much the heavier of the two, should test it first. He did so, with the result that the mattress collapsed, and his head became stuck between the ironwork. It was quite a work of art to get him out, and it was even a greater work of art to prop up the bed in such a way that we could use it. I remember another occasion when three of us – Murdoch, W.W.Read, and myself – had the luxury of reposing on a narrow table, while the rest had to sleep on the floor. I shall always remember one meal that we had. We were so ravenously hungry that our delight knew no bounds when we found that there was some boiled lamb to be had. The lamb was brought in triumph, but, to our sorrow we found that the establishment only boasted one knife and fork. We felt that we couldn't possibly wait to take turns with these, and so we had to do the best we could. The worst time that I experienced was when we were stuck in a river, and the light weights had to be carried across. Somebody called out to the nigger who was doing his best to get me across safely, 'Drop him in the river – he hasn't had such a chance of a bath for five days.' This, of course was quite true and from the way the nigger smiled I began to think that he would act on the advice.[173]

---

172   *Wisden Book of Test Cricket* (1979 edition) p 9
173   Bettesworth *Chats on the Cricket Field*   p 335

Cricket summed up the tour as follows:

> Though the financial result may not have been so satisfactory
> as its promoters could have wished, the tour of the English
> team to South Africa was, at all events, a complete success
> from a cricket standpoint. Of twenty matches thirteen were
> won and seven drawn. On paper the team was strong enough
> to give a good account of itself against any combination
> South Africa could produce, so that a defeat was hardly to be
> expected. Still, considering the difference of climate, the long
> and difficult journeys which had to be made in some cases,
> and the lavish hospitality they received everywhere, Mr Read
> and his comrades have reason to be more than satisfied with
> their cricket record....
>
> The chief features of the tour were the incredibly fine bowl-
> ing of Mr Ferris, and the consistent scores of Chatterton. With
> Martin, J.T.Hearne and Pougher, not to mention Alec Hearne
> in the team, there was plenty of variety in the attack, and Mr
> Ferris' figures, even allowing that the average of South African
> batting is not particularly high, were throughout the most
> noteworthy. Chatterton was essentially the safe man of the
> team as a run-getter. That he finally upheld his reputation as a
> thoroughly reliable batsman goes without saying.[174]

However successful the tour might have been in terms of results,
there can be no doubt that financially and legally, it verged on
disaster. It was always likely to be the case. The preceding
rugby tour had not helped and the imbalance in quality between
the English team and their hosts hardly made for competitive
cricket. Although stronger than Major Warton's 1888/89 team, it
was scarcely England's strongest. Lord Sheffield and W.G.Grace
led a simultaneous tour to Australia and Lord Hawke had a team
in the United States. George Ayres and Edwin Leaney had not
played first-class cricket; the latter was never to do so.

£750 had been advanced for the tour by James Logan, an
entrepreneur, philanthropist and passionate supporter of cricket,
though, as is usually the case with sponsors, his motives were
not 100% altruistic. It was unclear as to whether the advance was
a grant towards the expenses of the tour or a loan to be repaid
from the proceeds, which in the end were insufficient. Read
and Ash took the former view; Logan the latter – and, more

---

174   *Cricket* 14 April 1892

importantly, so did the Supreme Court in Cape Town. It all made for a colourful and dramatic departure.

> The tug left the Docks-side at half-past nine taking passengers and visitors and all the English cricketers with the exception of Messrs W W Read and Edwin Ash to the ship. Messrs Read and Ash arrived later in a rowing boat, having been detained in town on some business connected with the finance in connection with the tour...Messrs Read and Ash, hearing they were to be arrested stayed in town later than the remainder of the team yesterday morning in order to place themselves at the disposal of the Sheriff, and on being informed that the only way they could be released from arrest and allowed to proceed by the *Dunottar Castle* would be to deposit in the hands of the Court sufficient to cover the amount claimed or security for the same. This was done and they were permitted to depart. But an action in the matter is to come on in the Supreme Court in a few weeks or months hence when the claim will it is said be disputed.[175]

Bassano and Smith in their book on the tour say that searches through court archives for 1892 have failed to reveal any record of the case being brought before the courts and draw the conclusion that the parties settled their dispute privately. Not so. Not only in Hamlet's time was the law's delay something which had to be borne...The case eventually came to court in June of the following year, when the *South African Sportsman* summarised the verdict in the following scorecard.

SINGLE WICKET MATCH
Played at the Supreme Court, Cape Town on Tuesday June 7, 1893
Gentlemen of England

W W Read c Sir H de Villiers b J D Logan		0
W L Murdoch	run out	0
'Daddy' Ash	retired hurt	0
Mr Bridgette	absent	0

Total		0

J D Logan not out	750
Extras	107

Innings declared closed	857

The significance of the tour in Read's own mind is perhaps encapsulated by the single line in Annals of Cricket at the end of his entry for 1891: 'In the winter of this year I captained a team out to South Africa'.[176] Furthermore, there is no mention of Read's absence or his achievements in the Surrey minutes, suggesting that even though the massacre in Cape Town was subsequently deemed a Test match, the tour ranked below county cricket and international cricket against Australia in the eyes of both the England captain and his county club.

Lord Alverstone, earlier Sir Richard Webster, with whom Read conducted his contractual negotiations.
[Surrey County Cricket Club]

---

176   *Annals of Cricket* p 184

Chapter Nine
Negotiations…no broken Read, he

The testimonial match against England in 1895 was meant to signal if not the end, then certainly the beginning of the end of Walter Read's first-class playing career. He did not go quietly, the discussions were prolonged over almost three years, involving a number of members of the Surrey hierarchy and his negotiating skills were demonstrated to the full.

The saga began as early as February 1894 when John Shuter approached the Committee with the suggestion of a testimonial match. In October of the same year, it had been agreed that there should be one, but with an important proviso.

> It was arranged that a complimentary match be arranged for Mr W W Read in 1895 and that if possible Surrey and England be played and that the Secretary be instructed to approach the other Counties on the subject. It was resolved that it be an understanding in the arrangement between the Committee and Mr W W Read that the Assistant Secretaryship of the Club come to an end on his ceasing to be a member of the Surrey Eleven.[177]

There was absolutely no pretence that the Assistant Secretaryship was anything other than a device to enable him to play cricket full-time and be paid for it, though Read was clearly unwilling to consider the termination of either, nor any other arrangement, notwithstanding a firm resolution by the Committee before the start of the 1895 season.

> It was resolved that Mr Read be informed that the existing arrangement between the Club and him would cease at the end of the year and that the question of any further arrangement for the future could then be considered.[178]

The Club's publicity machine was mobilised. Every member received a letter from the Secretary in the following terms:

---

177   Surrey CCC minutes 18 October 1894
178   Surrey CCC minutes 21 March 1895

April 18th 1895

Dear Sir

MR W W READ'S TESTIMONIAL MATCH
SURREY v ENGLAND
OVAL MAY 27TH 28TH AND 29TH

The Committee invite the co-operation of the members generally in their endeavours to make this testimonial to Mr WALTER READ a success in every way. Subscriptions to this end may be sent to the Secretary.

By order
Yours faithfully
C W Alcock
Secretary

The match left Read over £800 better off (Bobby Abel's benefit match in the same season yielded £200 less) but he was still determined to hang on as long as possible.

At the end of the season, a sub-committee comprising the President, Vice-President, Captain and Secretary, having discussed Mr Read's position with him recommended:

> that in their opinion it was fair to Mr Read that the present arrangement as to the Assistant Secretaryship should be continued as long as Mr Read continues to be a regular member of the Surrey eleven. The Assistant Secretaryship to be deemed to commence on the 1st of January in each year and the salary of Assistant Secretary to be paid to the 31st Decr in the year in which he shall cease to be a playing member.[179]

The usual courtesies were observed. Read wrote to the Committee at the beginning of the New Year.

Reigate Jan 16 1896

Dear Sirs

May I take this opportunity of thanking you for the many kindnesses you have extended to me during the many years I have been connected with Surrey Cricket especially for the testimonial and donation granted last season. You may rest assured that in future no effort on my part will be spared to

---

179   Surrey CCC minutes 21 November 1895

help the County to retain the proud position that it now holds.

> I remain, Dear Sirs,
> Yours faithfully
> W W Read

The velvet glove contained an iron fist. At the end of the season, shortly after the boat had been rocked by the professionals selected for England (Abel, Hayward, Lohmann and Richardson) for *inter alia* parity with the amateurs on pay, the Committee attempted to confirm and enforce that decision. Read was having none of it.

> I am quite at a loss to understand why any such proposed alteration be made, considering that during the present season I have been a regular member of the team and scored nearly 1000 runs, and besides having for the past fifteen or sixteen years, done more than any other member of the team to uphold the privilege of Surrey Cricket. I would suggest in all fairness both to yourselves and myself that the above mentioned office be continued at all events until December 31st 1897 upon the following terms viz:

> That the remuneration for the said office remains as heretofore £150 and railway season ticket and in addition to the extra payment of £100 and £4.4.0 for each match played which have been given to me in lieu of any increase in salary, these latter payments be made to me in the same proportions as the matches in which I take part.[180]

£375 was offered 'in lieu of all future payments'. It was declined. Not enough. The President of the Club, Sir Richard Webster QC, MP, later Lord Alverstone and Lord Chief Justice of England, got involved in the detail, bringing into play the razor-sharp legally trained mind one would expect in the Attorney-General which he was at this time. The correspondence closes with some cutting-edge negotiations, but once Webster was involved, Read was always going to come second. In the end £400 was then offered and accepted in full and final settlement, and the curtain fell on an illustrious career.

Following a meeting at the Attorney-General's chambers, having been accompanied by the Captain and Secretary (3-1 up and playing at home!), Sir Richard wrote:

---

180   Surrey CCC minutes 3 November 1896

28 October 1896

Dear Mr Read

In accordance with my promise of last evening I write to say that I am prepared to recommend the Committee of the Surrey Club to meet you on the basis proposed in your letter of 2 September – that your office of Assistant Secretary shall continue until 31 December 1897 and that you receive by 25 March 1897 £375 in lieu of all future payments for salary, season tickets, allowances and match money. I can only repeat what I said to you yesterday that it is, I am sure, the wish of every member of the Committee to deal with you as fairly as they possibly can consistent with the arrangements made in the autumn of 1895.

I am,
very truly yours,
R E Webster

W W thought he might be able to better than that. He could, but not by much.

14 November 1896

Dear Sir

Referring to your letter of 28 October and the interview with yourself, Mr Shuter and Mr Alcock at your rooms when you were good enough to say that you would kindly recommend to the Committee payments of such a sum of money as would be equal to such sums as I have been receiving from the Surrey Club in previous years. I would point out that £375 does not quite meet the case as you will see by the following – viz. £150 salary, £100 donation, £120 average match money, £28 season ticket – in all £398. I feel sure that you will not mind my placing the slight error before you.

With regard to the vexed question of the continuation of the Assistant Secretaryship I may say that never since my connection with the Surrey Club have I been told or has it been hinted to me, until I received the resolution passed by the Committee last summer, that the position was not to be permanent, otherwise it is most probable that I would have retired from Surrey cricket some time since.

As I am desirous after so many pleasant years of leaving with every feeling of satisfaction I would, with all respect to the Committee, suggest that some form of compromise should be arranged in lieu of my discontinuing the Assistant Secretaryship. With regard to what amount the Committee may think fair, I must of course leave that entirely in their hands.

Trusting that I may receive a favourable reply.

> I am dear Sir
> Yours faithfully
> W W Read

Incisively, the President replied:

> 2 Pump Street
> Temple EC
> 25 November 1896

Dear Mr Read

I brought your letter of the 14th and our previous correspondence before the committee and have received authority to arrange with you a payment of £400 by 25 March 1897 in satisfaction of all future payments from the Surrey to you.

This payment is made on the understanding that the Surrey Club are able to claim your assistance for all the First XI matches next year in which they desire you to play.

With reference to your request that some further amount be paid you in consideration of your discontinuing to be Assistant Secretary, the Committee do not see their way to making any further payment. I must point out to you that the sum named (£400) is in excess of that which you were willing to receive according to your letter of 2nd September last inasmuch as you proposed that the extra payment of £100 and the fee for each match of 4 guineas should be contingent on the number of matches played, whereas the Committee are now agreeing to pay you at once not only the full £100, but a sum which represents 4 guineas for each first eleven match of the season.

I feel sure that you will feel the Committee have met you in a friendly spirit.

> I am yours faithfully
> Richard E Webster

Anything else would be nit-picking. Maintaining his dignity, Read took the money, made himself available for another season and ran.

Micklefield, Reigate
Dec 6 1896

Dear Sir

I am much obliged to you for your letter of 25 November, the contents of which I have given due consideration, and I am quite prepared to accept the terms proposed by the Committee of the Surrey CCC.

Apologising for not writing to you before and thanking you for the trouble you have taken in the matter.

Believe me,
Yours faithfully
W W Read

The minutes record a payment of £400 to Read on 1 April 1897. The curtain had only a few inches to drop.

Chapter Ten
Annals of Cricket and Short Hints on Cricket

In 1896, Read published his book Annals of Cricket, a somewhat unbalanced, pot pourri of a collection of writing, and unstirred mixture of fact and fantasy which according to its verbose title purports to be

A RECORD OF THE GAME COMPILED FROM
AUTHENTIC SOURCES
AND
MY OWN EXPERIENCES DURING THE LAST TWENTY-THREE
YEARS
BY
W.W.READ
For many years a Member of the Surrey County Team

WITH AN INTRODUCTION
BY
JOHN SHUTER
LATE
Captain Surrey County Eleven

John Shuter's Introduction is suitably eulogistic, recalling Read's qualities and achievements as a batsman, fielder, bowler and general all-round 'good egg'. He makes the requisite allusions to the two tours of Australia, the Test century in 1884, the consecutive double centuries in 1887 and the 338 in 1888, mentions his competence in the field and occasional successes as a 'lob-bowler', especially his 'hat-trick' at Scarborough in 1891 before going on to the Read personality.

> I cannot conclude this brief sketch without a short reference to Mr. Read's personal character both on and off the cricket-field. In spite of his wonderful successes he has ever maintained the same modest and unassuming manner which has made him a host of friends. Always cheerful and ready to make the best of a bad position, with a temper that nothing can ruffle,

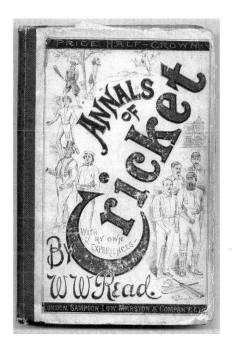

Cover of Annals of Cricket.

he is a model of what a cricketer on the field should be. Off the cricket-field, only those intimately acquainted with him can appreciate his genuine uprightness and unselfishness, and his characteristic good temper and geniality.

No one invited to write an Introduction to a book written by a friend is going to be over-critical, but although there were perhaps exceptions in Read's career to the affable equanimity that Shuter outlines here, on the whole he seems to have summed up the essence of the man.

The early part of the book is an attempt to trace something of the history and development of the game, but it is mainly from secondary sources of questionable reliability and lacks academic rigour. Locating the antecedents of the game in Greece, Rome and Persia, linked with contemporary attempts to revive the 'Olympian games', requires, as Read admits, a suspension of disbelief, and the cartoon-type sketches of Ancient Britons playing an early version of cricket with a club for the bat, a stone for the ball and a tree for the wicket owe more to a lively imagination than historical evidence and suggest that, despite protestations to the contrary, the author did not see himself as a serious cricket historian.

He is on more reliable ground with his descriptions of mediaeval bat and ball games and eighteenth-century cricket, but it is evident that, as he admits in the 'Author's Note', in days long before *Cricket Archive* was a twinkle in the eye of dedicated and computer-literate statisticians, his main purpose is something of an ego-trip and is to provide a permanent record of his achievements on the field and his own comments on them. He surveys the game from its alleged beginnings, through its manifestation in a more recognisable form, beginning a new chapter for 1873 to mark his own arrival on the first-class scene. From that point, he has the advantage of being an eye-witness of and at times a participant in the history which he is recording. At the beginning of Chapter VI, he writes:

> In placing the present year under the heading of a fresh chapter, I had in mind the fact that it was my first introduction to the public in good-class cricket, and I possess the feeling that from now almost all I have to write about is either taken from actual observation, or a thorough knowledge of the circumstances under which it transpired.....

> When I started at the Oval it was in the match Surrey v. Yorkshire.... Being young and green I was very slow, and I shall never forget the advice given me by that veteran Henry Jupp, who remarked: "Now, young man, look here! The first thing you have to do if you want to be a cricketer is to keep your wicket up, and the runs are sure to come." The value of such admonition from one of the leading professionals of the day was present to my mind for years afterwards, and I commend the advice as it stands to all young aspirants of the game.

Aided by early Surrey statistician Anthony Benitez de Lugo, he lists all his own innings against each opponent, centuries, wicket-keeping and bowling performances and provides supplementary information on the personnel and results of Australian and other tours, and some statistics on the Eton v Harrow and Varsity matches. He lists players he has played with and against and provides illustrations of the evolution of cricket dress and equipment. It all seems a little quaint these days, but at the time, the book was as comprehensive a record as anything produced outside the *Wisden* and *Lillywhite* publications.

It was seriously trailed in *Cricket* and elsewhere, sold at 2/6 per copy with a de luxe edition at 10/6 on hand-made paper, numbered and signed. It contained thirty illustrations, including a portrait of the author. The book clearly proved popular. Within a year a 1/- 'paperback' edition had appeared.

> ..of cricket books just now there is apparently no ending which is hardly to be wondered at with the season at its height. Mr W W Read's "Annals of Cricket" have reached a shilling edition, substantial proof of their popularity.[181]

An earlier less substantial publication was *Short Hints on Cricket,* even shorter and less substantial than the title suggests. They occupy just eight small pages of what is little more than a pamphlet the main purpose of which is to act as a catalogue for the goods of W.H.Cook & Co Ltd, Cricket Bat Manufacturers of 297 Victoria Park Road. London NE (now E9). W.H. Cook was Managing Director, Read was Chairman and the remaining Directors were Dr W.G. Grace, A.N.Hornby, A.J.Webbe, Rt Hon Lord Hawke, J.Shuter and A.Wells, with one exception, distinguished first-class cricketers, and two exceptions, educated at Eton, Harrow or Winchester. Grace was not public school educated and Wells was neither public school educated, nor a first-class cricketer. He was, however, the father-in-law of the Chairman, a self-made man and by this time a

W. W. R.   D. McD.

ANCIENT BRITONS AT PLAY.

(With apologies to Mr. E. T. Reed.)

Early cricket - as Read envisaged it might have been.

181   *Cricket* 8 July 1897

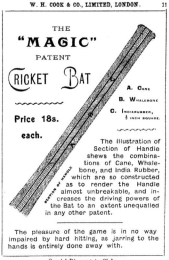

Advertisement for the 'Magic' bat.

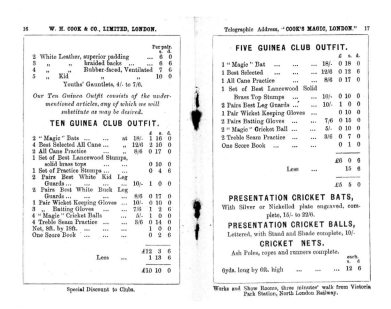

W.H.Cook & Co's price list for cricket gear.

gentleman, though clearly a man with a track record of business success and some technical expertise in India rubber which along with cane and whalebone was a major component of the handle of the 'Magic' Patent cricket bat, Cook's flagship and heavily advertised product. Whether Walter had met Florence as a result of his involvement with Arthur Wells or vice versa is unclear, but the two men clearly formed a potentially strong business partnership.

It is doubtful whether the Board of Directors actually met. The likelihood is that, possibly in return for an honorarium and a few free bats, they were agreeable to lending their names to an endorsement of a piece of equipment eulogised in the preface to the price list in the following terms.

> In directing the attention of the Cricketing Public to the following Price List of a few of the articles we manufacture and trade in, we may state that we purposefully refrain from the usual course of publishing testimonials in favour of our specialties, feeling sure that cricketers will attach more importance to the fact that our Patent "MAGIC" Bat has been found to possess sufficient merit to attract the attention and secure the patronage of some of England's most eminent players, a few of whom comprise our Board of Directors.

> The fact that some of these gentlemen have previously testified to the good qualities of other patent bats (all of which they have now relinquished) conclusively proves that, as a weapon of cricketing warfare, the "MAGIC" is unequalled. Such testimony, we think, will be sufficient recommendation to all lovers of the National Game to try the "MAGIC" Bat, which we confidently predict will speedily supersede all other patents and drive IMITATIONS out of the market.[182]

It didn't of course, despite the endorsements and aggressive salesmanship. Apart from thirteen pages of advertising and price lists, there are nine pages on the Laws of Cricket (some of them still uncut in 125 years in the copy of this rare pamphlet held in the Lord's Library!) plus a couple for the insertion of 'Engagements' and 'Results', and a quarter of this small publication is dedicated to what the title suggests, short hints on cricket, though mainly on batting with a bit on fielding and nothing on bowling. Some are timeless, some are dated, others a mixture of the two.

---

182   *Short Hints on Cricket* p9

On forward play, for instance, he advises:

> The great secret of placing the left leg across the wicket when playing forward is that the left leg is taken so close to the bat, that it is impossible for the ball to get between it and the bat.

That technique is still sound today, though his suggestion that driving be restricted to half-volleys has been succeeded by the method of sensibly using the feet to make a good length ball into the required half-volley.

> It is impossible to drive any other ball than a "half-volley", though very often the batsman (by running out of his ground) tries to make many deliveries of the bowler of this particular ball, and not a few times in a season comes to grief. I strongly advise the reader to cultivate this style of play but at the same time not to be too reckless.

Although Read is credited with, if not inventing at least developing, the pull shot, he makes no specific mention of it, but does expand on 'leg-hitting' both in front and square of the wicket.

> This is a very useful stroke, especially now that the field is placed so much on the off-side, but is not so often indulged in as in years back, probably because one gets, in really good cricket, so few balls on the leg side. A batsman to put himself into a position for a long leg[183] hit must place his left leg well forward in a line with his right, the knee slightly bent so that he might strike the ball directly it leaves the pitch. To make a square leg hit the batsman has to be in an entirely different position, as the left leg must be drawn back to the right and the body turned directly facing the bowler. The only ball that a batsman is able to make this hit from with safety is an over pitched ball directly on to his legs, though not by any means a "yorker".

Modern coaching would suggest placing the front foot wider and opening up the body for the on drive, and the cross-batted shot through square leg can be played to a short-pitched ball of any length, but we are still almost half a century from 'leg theory' and the 'hints' are sound enough to encourage aspiring cricketers to acquire the pamphlet and perhaps buy themselves a 'magic' bat and other cricket equipment.

---

183   i e long on

There can be no doubt about his credentials to comment on batting technique.

> As a match-winner, the county never had a better batsman. He was a wonderful punishing player, with tremendous power in his off drive.

> More forward in style than most of the great batsmen of the present time, he was seen at his best on true lively wickets, but he came off under all conditions of ground and weather... In his young days Mr Read could be described as an orthodox player, depending as he did on his driving and the perfect straightness of his bat; but as time went on he developed a great fondness for pulling. He carried the pull to a higher pitch than anyone else in his day, but from being a good servant, the stroke became, to some extent, his master and impaired his batting. That at least was the opinion of Mr Shuter than whom he had no warmer admirer.[184]

However, his record is distinguished enough to suggest that he was far from being a one-trick pony.

The advice on running between the wickets is universally valid –

> The batsman should always run the first run fast, in case the fieldsman should not pick up the ball cleanly, and he should lose the opportunity of making another.

– while that on fielding reflects the contemporary attitude that it was a chore to be endured between innings before players like Abel and Lohmann developed it into more of an art form.

> It would be well for my reader to pay special attention to this pleasing but much neglected part of the game, and to practise it with a determination that no stone may be upturned to make himself a clean and safe field... To make one's self a good field is, perhaps, the most irksome part of cricket, for it can only be done by really hard work...

> Never throw hard unless there is a chance of running a man out as it only tends to tire the wicket keeper , bowler and fieldsman – frequently results in runs for your opponents.

One would hope that wicket-keepers, bowlers and fieldsmen tire less easily these days.

---

184   *Surrey Mirror* 11 January 1907

Chapter Eleven

Last Years

In 1899, Bobby Abel passed the individual Surrey record established by Read eleven years before. In the meantime, Archie MacLaren's 424 for Lancashire against Somerset had replaced Grace's 344 as the highest individual score. Despite the feigned resentment, there can be no doubt that the congratulatory telegram was sincere. From his writings, it appears Read had a good relationship with the professionals and there is no evidence to the contrary elsewhere.

> Abel, Kennington Oval, You Brute, hearty congratulations, Walter Read.[185]

Read was far from inactive in his retirement from active cricket and despite an attachment to 'cupola' continued to play cricket.

> It is said that Mr W W Read has lately taken to playing Cupola, a new game of the variety which does not demand much running from its devotees, and that he has expressed his approval of it. This is very sad for we are afraid it is likely to lead to other things in the way of quiet games, and one day we may wake up to find the famous old cricketer has become the champion of croquet. As, however, he still plays cricket we must hope for the best.[186]

In 1900, he stood for the Committee, but was last in the poll. He came tenth out of ten with 50 votes, Kingsmill Key, Clifton and Oxford, who had given up the captaincy at the end of the previous season, topped the poll with 118.

However, in 1905 after an unsuccessful venture into estate agency and auctioneering with his brother-in-law, Frederick Wells, he returned to the club, as Instructor, at a salary of £150 per annum, less than he had received as a player, but possibly more than he was making from his auctioneering, and he was in a job in which he probably felt more at home. He succeeded W.T.Graburn as coach to the young players of whom Jack Hobbs, the young

---

185   *Life and Reminiscences of Bobby Abel* p 110
186   *Cricket* 10 August 1899

Cambridge player, now qualified for Surrey, was one. He was described by *Cricket* as 'promising',[187] a shrewd judgment given that the young man in question was to score more first-class centuries than anyone else in the history of the game

Read's reports, detailed and conscientious, reflect the approach of one who took his duties seriously.

> In accordance with instructions I have seen the following Colts and beg to report as follows:
>
> J.W. Hitch Born in Lancashire, Age 19. Fast right hand bowler and distinctly good. I would strongly recommend that he be taken on the Ground Staff for the purpose of qualifying. Jacobs, age 19. Qualified by residence, a decidedly good right hand medium paced bowler and capable of much improvement. I would recommend that he be taken on the ground staff for the purpose of 2nd XI and C & G matches. Gamble, born in Leics, is a really good medium pace left hand bowler and will, I think. be invaluable in C & G matches and well worth qualifying.
>
> Meads [sic] so far as I have seen him appears to be a good bat and bowler and should be played as often as possible... Stagg is a good bat and a steady bowler. Crossley a good right hand bowler. Henderson a poor bat and bowler left hand medium. Abel jr a decidedly good bat and fair bowler etc ...etc ...These I would advise playing as often as possible.... There were no other Colts that had any pretensions to become first-class cricketers...
>
> In accordance with instructions I have attended matches at Leatherhead and Epsom...with regard to the staff generally I may safely say they are improving.[188]

Abel jr and Hitch played first-class cricket, but none of the others did, except of course Battersea-born Philip Mead who went off to carve himself a career with Hampshire.

Sadly, the appointment lasted just two seasons. Walter Read died of pneumonia at his home in Addiscombe Park after a period of indifferent health at the young age of 51 on Sunday 6 January 1907. Charles Alcock and Edward Pooley, both distinguished servants of the club in different ways were to follow later in the year. The President and Henry Leveson-Gower made the necessary

---

187   *Cricket* 27 April 1905
188   4 & 18 May 1905

arrangements for a testimonial fund for his widow and family which remained open till the end of the season.[189]

His funeral was held at Shirley in Croydon four days after his death, and although a private affair was attended by members of the family (only the male ones; it was not the practice for women to attend funerals at this time) and representatives from the world of cricket and commerce. One significant absentee was Charles Alcock, his boss at The Oval during the time of the Assistant Secretaryship, himself in his final illness. Floral tributes were numerous.

His grave is in the churchyard of St John the Evangelist, Shirley. It consists of an upright stone Celtic cross and is simply inscribed: In ever loving memory of Walter William Read, died Jan 6th 1907 aged 51 years. Peace, Perfect Peace. On the side is added: Also his wife Florence, died October 14th 1935 aged 76 years. O Perfect Love.[190] So, Florence's death was very nearly fifty years after the wedding, 21 years of marriage being followed by almost 29 of widowhood.

Among a number of Obituaries, *Cricket* said

> For 25 years Mr Read played first-class cricket and for at least ten years of that time no Eleven could have been chosen to represent England unless it included him in its ranks.

> From 1883 to 1893 may be the decade referred to, and in some of those years he was bracketed with Shrewsbury as second only to "W G".[191]

Five years after his death, he remained an iconic figure. On the death of George Bonnor, J.N. Pentelow, now Editor of *Cricket* wrote

> So the mighty Bonnor has passed to the Elysian fields, where a friend of mine pictures Johnny Briggs and George Lohmann and William Murdoch and Walter Read taking wickets and

---

189   Surrey CCC minutes 16 May & 5 September 1907
190   The epitaphs sound biblical. In fact both are from the first lines of hymns, Walter's from Edward Henry Bickersteth, Bishop of Exeter 1885-1900, which concludes:
It is enough: earth's struggles soon shall cease,
And Jesus call us to heaven's perfect peace.
and Florence's from Dorothy Frances Gurney's wedding hymn, first used at the marriage of Princess Louise of Wales and the Duke of Fife in 1889, and has an almost parallel ending:
...the glorious unknown morrow
That dawns upon eternal love and life.
Whether the family had this coincidence in mind is a matter of speculation, but maybe like Walter and Florence, it is something approaching a perfect fit
191   *Cricket* 31 January 1907

scoring runs as on earth.[192]

C.B.Fry described 'the great WW' as 'a burly, heavy-shouldered ex-schoolmaster, with an oblong brown face and quick, rather cunning brown eyes'.[193] Read was clearly a well-rounded sportsman: of international quality as a batsman, he could field anywhere, was more than an occasional wicket-keeper and his lob bowling was not the worst.

Writing on 'Ashes' captains, for which Read qualifies on the basis of one game when no one knew or cared whether the Ashes were at stake anyway, Gerry Cotter writes,

> Read was an interesting character, a bluff and dashing extrovert who never worried about whom he upset......His assertive personality had some merits as a captain and he knew his cricket well enough. With other more outstanding players about he was never going to lead England very often but one has the feeling that he might have made quite a good captain had he had more opportunity.[194]

Surrey spin paints a rather more mellow character.

> He was ever a most genial companion, and I can truthfully say that during all the years I was playing with him nothing ever upset his unfailing good temper on the cricket field and nothing occurred to mar our association off it.[195]

W.G.Grace, concentrating more on his batting technique, than his character and temperament, summed him up as follows.

> Mr. Walter William Read was born at Reigate, Surrey, on the 23rd November, 1855. His height is 5ft, 11½ in; weight 14st.5lbs. He will stand out as one of the great batsmen of the age. For excellent defence and vigorous hitting he has had few equals; and today, though in his 36th year, his form is almost up to his best years. As far as I can learn, he had no special training, but his innate love for the game and unwearied perseverance brought him rapidly to the front. He was tried by the Surrey Committee at the early age of 17. His defence was excellent then; and great things were predicted of him when he reached the years of manhood. He always played with a straight bat, and as the years went on and strength came, his hitting

192   Cricket 6 July 1912
193   Fry *Life Worth Living* p 142
194   Cotter *The Ashes Captains* p41
195   John Shuter in *Surrey Cricket, its History and Associations* p 214

powers improved rapidly. For quick scoring he has few equals, and there is no one the cricket-loving public watches with greater delight.

The very first over he is on the alert for a loose ball, and I do not envy the bowler when he has got well set. Like most of our great batsmen, he has his pet hits. A long hop on the off-side is his especial delight. He makes no attempt to pull it to the on, as one or two powerful hitters do, but steps back with his right foot, and smites terrifically hard between point and mid-off. He plays every ball clean and hard, however good the length of it, and on the leg side he is exceptionally strong in placing. Of late years he has fielded close in, but he is also good in the long-field; and it is an open secret that he can keep wicket fairly well, and bowls lobs at a pinch. In 1881, for Surrey v Yorkshire at Huddersfield, he kept wicket while Yorkshire scored 388 and did not give a single extra.[196]

The division between amateur and professional, though apparently clear-cut was blurred at the edges. For landed gentry, playing the game for recreation, making money from it was, in most cases, an irrelevance. They didn't need it. For the professionals, the hired labourers and working classes of the game, it was supremely relevant. They did need it. In the middle, straddling the dividing line, was an amorphous, not too well defined group, who could not afford to play regularly purely for the love of the game. Some – like Edward Pooley, George Lohmann and Ernest Hayes – from middle class backgrounds avoided the hypocrisy of shamateurism and threw in their lot with the professionals, in Lohmannn's case, doing much to enhance the status and respectability of the professional cricketer. Edwin Diver is an interesting example of one who started as an amateur and, against family opposition, transferred to the professional ranks. The dilemma for W.G.Grace and W.W.Read was that, financially, they could not afford to be amateurs and socially, could not afford to be professionals. Between them, however, they demonstrated that, if thick-skinned enough to deflect the criticism of those who objected to the paid amateur ethos, it was possible to have it all, to make a reasonable living from the game while retaining their social status of gentlemen and the privileges of amateurs.

Rev R.S.Holmes, with a Utopian vision of a more egalitarian society, took the moral high ground.

---

196   *Cricket* p 361

In sport the words *amateur* and *gentleman* are identical in meaning...A *professional* is one who plays at sport for a livelihood...*Either every man who makes money by sport is a professional, or no man is.* It is the snobbishness of the disguised professional I protest against.[197]

Keith Sandiford, using supporting material from the *Athletic News* summed up the position of the middle group by saying that many gentlemen were unable to play regularly without payment of some kind and that "it was also beneath their dignity to play for wages or to use the same facilities as the professionals". Some, like Read, accepted payment of one kind or another thus earning more than the professional without losing their amateur status. Sandiford goes on to say that

The *Athletic News* spoke for the majority when, in 1879 it declared: Both cricketers and the public have become tired of the abuse of terms which confers upon one man the title of gentleman and upon another that of a professional, when the only difference between them is that the so-called gentleman takes money when he has no right to, and the professional who honestly calls himself such finds himself outbidden at his business by the mercenary amateur, who repudiates the title of professional whilst appropriating all the emoluments connected therewith.[198]

While the criticism, both contemporary and subsequent, of shamateurism and veiled professionalism, is entirely understandable and, indeed, justified, attitudes have to be seen in the context of sport and society which have changed beyond recognition between the late nineteenth century and the early twenty-first. Top class sport is now almost entirely professional, the standards of skill and professionalism now required are such that there is no longer room for the gifted amateur and the FA Amateur Cup, amateur international rugby union, amateur Wimbledon and amateur Olympic Games have disappeared with the twentieth century. Different sports have dealt with the metamorphosis from amateur to professional sport in different ways, association football by recognising professionalism early, rugby splitting into two separate codes. The Gaelic Athletic Association, staunchly amateur since its foundation in 1884, is now grappling with professionalism and may have reached

---

197   *Cricket* 11 April 1895
198   *Cricket and the Victorians* p 83

what an Editorial in the *Irish Times* called the 'final frontier of amateurism'.[199] Cricket, until 1963 existed in an uneasy symbiosis between amateur and professional with separate hotels, separate dressing rooms, separate gates and initials differently positioned on scorecards.

Society too has changed: the rise of organised labour from its nineteenth century origins; the erosion of the class system in the twentieth, especially after the First World War; the subsequent blurring of a class-based political system to the point where the two parties which, led by Gladstone and Disraeli, opposed each other through the nineteenth century, are in coalition government in the twenty-first....all this was not foreseen by Walter Read and his contemporaries.

Class was significant. There were broadly three – aristocracy, middle-class and working-class – but subdivisions within each and movement, usually upwards between the lower two. Other than by marriage or inheritance, movement to the aristocracy was not an option. Fuelled by Mechanics' Institutes, Education Acts and an ethos of self-improvement epitomised by the plethora of schools in Reigate, those in the middle-class, whether by birth or upward social mobility were, like Walter Read, reluctant to surrender that social advantage. Dr Donna Loftus writes,

> The economic boundary of the 'middle-class' was not clear. Some members of the middle-class used their wealth to buy land and stately homes, becoming as rich, if not richer than the aristocracy. At the same time, many members of the skilled working class could earn as much if not more than some members of the lower middle-class.[200]

A well-known sketch on the BBC's *Frost Programme* in the following century when the class system was breaking down, but still present, puts the situation in comic, but no less graphic, terms.

Three men, of decreasing heights and parallel decreasing social status stand in a line and say:

> "I have got innate breeding, but I have not got any money. So sometimes I look up to him." (the middle-class man)

> "I still look up to him, because although I have money, I am vulgar. But I am not as vulgar as him (the lower-class man). So

199   27 March 2010
200   Loftus *The Rise of the Victorian Middle Classes* Open University 2010

I still look down on him"

"I know my place. I look up to them both. But while I am poor, I am industrious, honest and trustworthy. Had I the inclination, I could look down on them."[201]

Who was Who 1897-1915 records biographical details of significant people who died between those years. W.G.Grace, some have said the best known Victorian apart from the Queen herself and Gladstone, is there, so is C.W.Alcock, Secretary of the FA and Surrey County Cricket Club for more than three decades. Absent are George Lohmann and Tom Richardson, bowlers and professionals, who between them played in 32 Test Matches, contributing to victories in most of them. Walter Read, batsman and amateur, who played in eighteen, is there.

We live in an age when the great-great granddaughter of a coal-miner can be married to the second in line to the throne. That would not have been possible in Read's day when deference was an accepted part of Victorian society. But limited social mobility was possible and encouraged. Class mattered and Walter William Read was determined to establish, maintain and improve his position in the social structure of his time.

Read's grave at St. John's Church, Shirley.

---

201   Played by John Cleese, Ronnie Barker and Ronnie Corbett. *Daily Telegraph* 6 November 2010

Acknowledgements

Bridgeman Art Gallery and the executors of the estate of the late Hazel Radcliffe-Dolling for permission to reproduce the painting by G.H.Barrable and R.Ponsonby Staples.

Jo Miller for her unfailing help in providing access to the facilities of the Surrey Cricket Library – as well as numerous cups of tea and several varieties of confectionery.

Andy Packham, President, Reigate Priory Cricket Club for help with the early records of the club and permission to reproduce the portrait of Walter Read and the photograph of the 1894 W.W. Read's XI v W.G.Grace's XI match.

Philip Paine for providing the photograph of Walter Read's grave and permission to reproduce it.

Mike and Neil Read for information on the family, permission to reproduce the photographs of the clock presented by the Surrey Club to Walter as a wedding present and the scroll commemorating the 1882/83 tour of Australia; and to Neil for the sample of his great grandfather's handwriting and for kindly agreeing to write the Foreword.

Neil Robinson, MCC Research Officer, for unearthing a rare copy of Read's *Short Hints on Cricket*.

Surrey County Cricket Club for permission to reproduce team photographs, extracts from Committee minutes and correspondence, the scorebook of the 1884 Test match at The Oval and the scorecard of Read's triple-century against Oxford University.

Roger Mann for his help with pictures.

Ken Sutherland of the Redhill Centre for Local and Family History for his researches into the Read and Wells families.

Peter Wynne-Thomas for access to his index of *The Cricketer*.

My wife, Jennifer, for her diligent research, particularly into nineteenth century Reigate, and her assiduous checking of drafts and proofs, preparing the family tree and statistics and unwavering support throughout the whole project.

David Jeater, series editor, and Roger Moulton who has edited this particular book.

Gerald Hudd and Jenny Moulton for their proofreading.

Richard Shaw and all those at City Press for typesetting and printing.

Thanks are also due to the following for their help in making their facilities available:
British Newspaper Library
MCC
Surrey History Centre
Surrey County Cricket Club

Appendix A
Chronology

1855	Born in West Street, Reigate
1869	Début for Reigate Priory Cricket Club
1871	Assistant Teacher at Holmesdale House
1873	Début for Surrey
1877	First plays in Gentlemen v Players fixture
1879	First Reigate Priory Cricket Week
1881	Appointed Assistant Secretary to Surrey County Cricket Club
1882/83	Début for 'England' on Ivo Bligh's tour of Australia
1885	*Short Hints on Cricket* Marries Florence Wells in Reigate
1887	Consecutive double-centuries
1887/88	Tours Australia with G.F.Vernon. Captains 'England' in only Test
1888	338 v Oxford University
1891/92	Captains 'England' in South Africa
1893	Resurrects Reigate Priory Cricket Week
1896	*Annals of Cricket*
1897	Retires from first-class cricket
1905	Appointed as 'Instructor' by Surrey
1907	Dies in Addiscombe; buried in the churchyard of St John the Evangelist, Shirley

Appendix B – Seven Generations of Reads

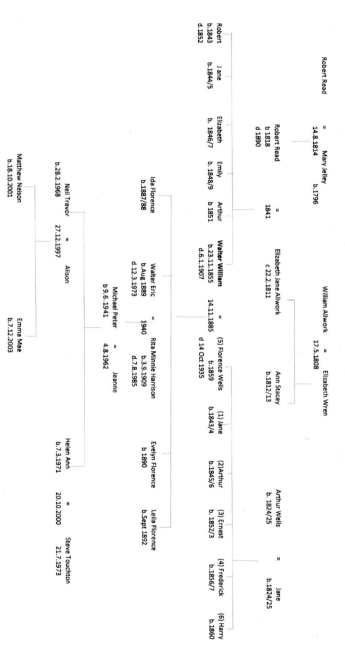

Appendix C
Career Statistics

Test Cricket: Batting and Fielding

		M	I	NO	R	HS	Ave	100	50	Ct
1882/83	Australia	4	7	0	228	75	32.57	-	2	1
1884	Australia	2	2	0	129	117	64.50	1	-	2
1886	Australia	3	4	0	176	94	44.00	-	2	3
1887/88	Australia	1	2	0	18	10	9.00	-	-	2
1888	Australia	3	4	0	44	19	11.00	-	-	3
1890	Australia	2	4	0	21	13	5.25	-	-	1
1891/92	South Africa	1	1	0	40	40	40.00	-	-	-
1893	Australia	2	3	1	64	52	32.00	-	1	4
Totals		**18**	**27**	**1**	**720**	**117**	**27.69**	**1**	**5**	**16**

Test Cricket: Bowling

		O	M	R	W	BB	Ave	5i	10m
1882/83	Australia	8	2	27	0	-	-	-	-
1884	Australia	7	0	36	0	-	-	-	-
Total		**15**	**2**	**63**	**0**	**-**	**-**	**-**	**-**

First-class cricket: Batting and Fielding

	M	I	NO	R	HS	Ave	100	50	Ct	St
1873	2	4	0	56	39	14.00	0	0	2	
1874	2	4	0	20	16	5.00	0	0	1	
1875	5	10	2	247	98	30.87	0	1	3	
1876	9	17	3	588	106	42.00	1	3	3	
1877	7	11	0	399	140	36.27	1	2	3	
1878	8	15	3	278	80	23.16	0	1	3	
1879	5	6	0	123	53	20.50	0	1	3	
1880	6	12	0	306	93	25.50	0	1	6	
1881	16	30	1	931	160	32.10	1	6	13	6
1882	19	35	1	882	117	25.94	1	5	25	
1882/83	7	11	0	291	75	26.45	0	2	1	
1883	22	39	6	1573	168	47.66	2	13	37	12
1884	27	46	3	1256	135	29.20	2	5	37	
1885	27	42	0	1880	163	44.76	6	9	26	
1886	28	46	3	1825	120	42.44	4	12	29	
1887	23	36	2	1615	247	47.50	5	5	28	
1887/88	8	13	2	610	183	55.45	3	1	13	
1888	28	41	2	1414	338	36.25	4	3	24	
1889	20	33	1	805	115	25.15	1	4	11	
1890	30	48	2	1169	94	25.41	0	8	23	
1891	24	36	0	831	77	23.08	0	4	16	
1891/92	1	1	0	40	40	40.00	0	0	0	

1892	23	37	5	1088	196*	34.00	3	5	14	
1893	28	46	3	1377	147*	32.02	1	9	21	2
1894	27	37	3	824	161	24.23	1	4	17	
1895	25	34	1	767	111	23.24	1	3	10	
1896	29	43	5	863	112	22.71	1	4	9	
1897	11	16	4	291	86*	24.25	0	2	3	
Totals	**467**	**749**	**52**	**22349**	**338**	**32.06**	**38**	**113**	**381**	**20**

Note: Read was dismissed 339 times caught (45.26%), 276 times bowled (36.85%), 27 times stumped (3.60%), 35 times lbw (4.67%), 19 times run out (25.37%), hit wicket once and retired once.

First-class cricket: Bowling

	O	M	R	W	BB	Ave	5i	10m
1873								
1874								
1875	17.3	1	52	3	3-29	17.33	-	-
1876	23	8	69	0	-	-	-	-
1877	10	0	31	1	1-11	31.00	-	-
1878	21	6	47	0	-	-	-	-
1879	13	1	23	4	2-4	5.75	-	-
1880	128	23	301	4	1-17	75.25	-	-
1881	51	9	145	5	2-28	29.00	-	-
1882	51	16	115	1	1-27	115.00	-	-
1882/83	53	18	92	5	4-28	18.40	-	-
1883	77	16	202	4	1-10	50.50	-	-
1884	73	17	201	5	2-22	40.20	-	-
1885	82	33	181	4	2-58	45.25	-	-
1886	44	10	116	3	2-38	38.66	-	-
1887	96.3	20	233	11	2-18	21.18	-	-
1887/88	21	5	52	2	1-16	26.00	-	-
1888	122.1	30	319	9	2-16	35.44	-	-
1889	36	4	127	4	2-2	31.75	-	-
1890	72	18	171	8	4-27	21.37	-	-
1891	46	4	146	8	6-24	18.25	1	-
1891/92								
1892	62	6	211	6	3-59	35.16	-	-
1893	51	8	202	2	1-13	101.00	-	-
1894	10	0	57	2	1-11	28.50	-	-
1895	41	3	130	5	2-9	26.00	-	-
1896	91.2	16	247	12	4-32	20.58	-	-
1897	3	0	13	0	-	-	-	-
Total 4 ball overs	**883.1**	**213**	**3483**	**108**	**6-24**	**32.25**	**1**	**-**
5 ball overs	**412.4**	**59**						

Notes: He took his wickets at the rate of one per 51.82 balls and conceded runs at the rate of about 3 per over. Of his 108 wickets 32 were bowled (29.62%), 64 were caught (59.25%), 5 were lbw (4.62%), 6 were stumped (5.55%) and one hit wicket (0.92%). His best bowling return was 15.2 – 3 – 24 – 6 for the Gentlemen of England v Sherwin's Notts XI at Scarborough in 1891 which included the hat-trick.

First-Class cricket: Centuries (38)

Score	For	Opponent	Venue	Season
106	Surrey	Kent	Maidstone	1876
140	Surrey	Yorkshire	The Oval	1877
160	Surrey	Kent	Maidstone	1881
117	Surrey	Kent	The Oval	1882
168	Surrey	Hampshire	The Oval	1883
127	Surrey	Lancashire	Manchester	1883
117	England	Australia	The Oval	1884
135	Surrey	Gloucestershire	Clifton	1884
123	Surrey	Derbyshire	Derby	1885
163	Surrey	Sussex	The Oval	1885
159	Gentlemen	Players	The Oval	1885
101	Surrey	Sussex	Hove	1885
135	Surrey	Nottinghamshire	The Oval	1885
109	Surrey	Derbyshire	The Oval	1885
114	Surrey	Cambridge University	The Oval	1886
115	Surrey	Derbyshire	The Oval	1886
120	Surrey	Gloucestershire	Clifton	1886
102*	South	Australians	Hove	1886
118	Surrey	Oxford University	Oxford	1887
247	Surrey	Lancashire	Manchester	1887
244*	Surrey	Cambridge University	The Oval	1887
145	Surrey	Derbyshire	Derby	1887
100	Surrey	Kent	The Oval	1887
183	G.F. Vernon's XI	South Australia	Adelaide	1887/88
119	G.F. Vernon's XI	New South Wales	Sydney	1887/88
142*	G.F. Vernon's XI	Victoria	Melbourne	1887/88
109	Gentlemen of England	Australians	Lord's	1888
103	Surrey	Yorkshire	The Oval	1888
338	Surrey	Oxford University	The Oval	1888
171	Surrey	Sussex	The Oval	1888
115	Surrey	Middlesex	The Oval	1889
112	Surrey	Sussex	Hove	1892
196*	Surrey	Sussex	The Oval	1892
107	Surrey	Gloucestershire	Cheltenham	1892
147*	Surrey	Lancashire	Manchester	1893
161	Surrey	Yorkshire	The Oval	1894
111	Surrey	Sussex	Hove	1895
112	Surrey	Warwickshire	The Oval	1896

Bibliography

Newspapers and Periodicals

The Age
The Australasian
Athletic News
The Bulletin
Daily Telegraph
Cape Times
Cricket, A Weekly Record of the Game
Cricket Quarterly
The Cricketer
Irish Times
Moonshine
Punch
Reigate, Redhill, Dorking and Epsom Journal
South African Sportsman
Sporting Life
Surrey Mirror

Books and Articles

Abel, Bobby, *Life and Reminiscences of Bobby Abel* Cricket & Sports Publishers 1910
Altham, H.S., *A History of Cricket* Allen & Unwin 1962
Alverstone, Lord & Alcock, C.W., *Surrey Cricket: Its History and Associations* Longmans, Green and Co 1902
Bassano, Brian & Smith, Rick, *The Visit of Mr W W Read's 1891-92 English Cricket Team to South Africa* J.W.Mackenzie 2007
Berry, Scyld & Peploe, Rupert, *Cricket's Burning Passion Ivo Bligh and the Story of the Ashes* Methuen 2006
Bettesworth, W.A., *Chats on the Cricket Field* Merritt & Hatcher 1910
Booth, Keith, *His Own Enemy: The Rise and Fall of Edward Pooley* Belmont Books 2000
Booth, Keith, *The Father of Modern Sport: The Life and Times of Charles W Alcock* Parr's Wood Press 2002
Booth, Keith, *George Lohmann, Pioneer Professional* SportsBooks 2007
Bradbury, Anthony, *The Surrey Champion : amateur or professional?* The Cricketer October 1985
Brann, George, *The English Team in South Africa* The Cricket Field May 1892
Cashman, Richard, *The "Demon Spofforth"*, New South Wales University Press, 1990
Coldham, James, *Lord Harris* George Allen and Unwin 1983
Cotter, Gerry, *The Ashes Captains* Crowood Press 1989
Cowley, Brian (ed), *First-Class Records 1846-2000* Surrey County Cricket Club 2001
Dewar, Wm (ed,) *The Cricket Annual 1892* Frank Fawcett
Domesday Book: A Complete Translation Penguin 1992
Fry, C.B., *Life Worth Living*, Eyre & Spottiswoode, 1939
Grace, W.G., *Cricket* Arrowsmith 1891
Haygarth, Arthur, *Scores and Biographies Volumes XII and XIV* 1879 and 1895
Hawke, Lord, *Recollections and Reminiscences* Williams & Norgate 1924
Kynaston, David, *Bobby Abel, Professional Batsman*, Night Watchman Books 1982
James Lillywhite's Cricketers' Annual

Loftus, Dr Donna, *The Rise of the Victorian Middle Classes* Open University 2010
Murray, Bruce & Goolam, Vahed, *Empire and Cricket* University of South Africa 2009
Meredith, Anthony, *The Demon and the Lobster* Kingswood Press 1987
Palgrave, R.F.D., *Illustrated Handbook to Reigate* Kohler and Coombes 1860 (facsimile edition 1973)
Read, W.W., *Annals of Cricket* Sampson, Lowe, Marston & Company 1896
Read, W.W., *Short Hints on Cricket* W H Cook & Co Ltd 1885
Sandiford, Keith A.P., *Cricket and the Victorians* Scolar Press 1994
Sawyer, David A., *Century of Surrey Stumpers: The History of Surrey Wicketkeepers* Articulate Studio 2001
Wakley, B J. *Classic Centuries in the Test Matches between England and Australia* Nicholas Kaye, 1964
Who was Who 1897-1915
Wisden Cricketers'Almanack

Websites
www.cricketarchive.com
www.ancestry.co.uk
www.measuringworth.com
www.findmypast.co.uk

Censuses of Population 1841-1901

Index